Reading Alive!

Written and illustrated by Gwen Gawith
This new edition revised and updated by Pat Triggs

A & C Black · London

This edition first published in Great Britain 1999
by A & C Black (Publishers) Ltd
35 Bedford Row, London, WC1R 4JH.

This edition © 1999 A & C Black (Publishers) Ltd.
First edition © 1990. Reprinted 1991, 1993.
First published 1989 by Longman Paul Limited, New Zealand,
with the title *Reading Alive!* © 1989 Longman Paul Limited.

A cataloguing in publication (CIP) record for this book is
available from the British Library.
ISBN 0-7136-5135-0

Acknowledgement
The cover illustration is by Alison Dexter.

introduction

WHO?

Reading Alive! is intended for teachers to use with 8-11 year old children of all abilities but some of the activities could be used with seven-year-olds who are confident, independent readers.

WHAT?

Reading Alive! offers a selection of attractive, photocopiable activities that will help children develop as readers. The activities are ideal for use in guided group reading during time dedicated to literacy teaching. The majority of activities relate to the reading of fictional narrative but some could also be used with poetry. The activities are designed to:

✓ help create a lively reading environment in the class and to promote reading as an enjoyable activity;

✓ help readers articulate their responses by providing vocabulary, supportive frameworks, and opportunities to practise;

✓ encourage re-reading, thinking and analysis;

✓ stimulate discussion and expression of opinions, and develop an understanding that opinions need to be supported and justified with reference and quotation;

✓ encourage exchange of news and views about books and authors so that individuals read more, become familiar with the work of different writers and extend the range and variety of their reading.

WHY?

Once children can independently read simple texts, the aim is to help them become confident in tackling more complex and demanding texts in a variety of genres. This means helping them to recognise the nature of different reading tasks (*What sort of text is this?*); make connections with other things they have read (*Have I read anything like this before? Is this like the author's other books?*); and make connections with experiences (*Have I seen or done anything like that? Do I believe this? Have I felt like that?*). The increasingly confident reader also needs to develop and extend a range of skills and strategies for active reading, including picturing, predicting, revising hypotheses and expectations, questioning, evaluating, developing patience and stamina.

Underlying *Reading Alive!* is the belief that this development happens where readers share and refine their responses and understanding with others. The activities in this book are designed to support this process and to help readers experience the pleasures and rewards that come from investing effort, energy and emotion in reading.

Foreword

Reading Alive! is reissued in a new edition at a time when there is a sharp focus on teaching reading and writing, with the aim of raising standards of literacy in schools. A major part of this focus is the notion of dedicated time for literacy (at least an hour each day in the primary school) and, in England, a strongly recommended format (the Literacy Hour) for teachers to follow.

The activities in *Reading Alive!* fit extremely well with this approach. I believe you will find that these lively and imaginative materials, originally created by Gwen Gawith and groups of teachers in New Zealand, support exactly the sort of reader-centred and text-centred work you want to plan for guided and independent group work in literacy. To find out exactly how the activities match the National Literacy Strategy planning framework, turn to **Reading Alive! and the National Literacy Strategy** (pages 7-10).

As children move through the primary years, the challenge is to ensure continued progress and development in reading and writing. However, enabling children to read widely and confidently is easier said than done. We have all met children who don't know how to 'lose' themselves in a story, who have never seen books as a source of enjoyment; who, if they do read, restrict themselves to reassuring formula-written texts, or who give the thumbs-down to books with lots of description, slow beginnings, complex narratives or ambiguous endings. Even 'literary readers' can get stuck on a plateau, unable to move on to more challenging texts.

To make it possible for children to tackle more complex and demanding books alone and with confidence, they need opportunities to compare with others the meanings they have found, to validate their responses, and to discuss their ideas about how texts work. They need time to engage in the kind of talk that helps to clarify and refine what they think. This process of reflecting on what we read and how we read teaches us about reading and about ourselves as readers. *Reading Alive!* helps to create these opportunities. It provides supportive structures and also a sound basis for creating an environment in which literacy can flourish. For more on this, see **How to create readers** (pages 5-6).

The emphasis that has been placed on the role of literacy in raising standards in schools is valid and understandable. But it's also important to remember what literacy is for. I share Gwen Gawith's passionate belief that:

'the ability to read competently, confidently, flexibly and fluently is power. To choose not to exercise that option is your right. If you cannot do it, you do not have the option of choosing and your power in society is reduced.'

Becoming a reader implies more than attaining a recognised educational 'level'. It means feeling at home with texts of all kinds, understanding that there are as many different reading styles and strategies as there are purposes for reading, having power over what is read rather than being at its mercy, and having the means to exercise informed choices. It also means knowing that reading can be challenging. In retrospect it can be rewarding but the process is not without effort. The difficult trick teachers have to pull off is to enable young readers to make these discoveries about reading and to know that the rewards make their effort worthwhile. The materials in *Reading Alive!* are our contribution towards helping you conjure some reading magic in your classroom. It has worked for us; we hope it will for you.

Pat Triggs

How to use the activities and lists

THE ACTIVITIES

All the activity sheets, plus the **Student View of Reading: Questionnaire** (page 57) and the **Readership Award** certificate (page 59) can be photocopied for use in the classroom.

The activities can be used in a variety of ways. You will find some suggestions on the back of each activity sheet and you can check how the activities match with the teaching objectives identified in the National Literacy Strategy on pages 6-9. There is plenty of scope for you to change and develop a format to invent new activities.

The activity framework provides a teacher-like support while groups or individuals work independently. For guided group work, plan when you will spend time with a group to consolidate or extend learning, to monitor progress and do some formative assessment. For example:

① You could start a group off with an activity to establish basic concepts, build confidence and clarify what has to be done.

② You may want to return to the group to review what they have produced, encourage them to listen to and question one another; evaluate what they have produced either individually or collectively, reinforce the practice of referring to the text or consider ideas for further development.

③ A group may also need your input as they prepare to move to some sort of plenary report-back, publication or public performance arising from an activity.

The idea that the activity requires sharing and discussing is central. Talking can precede and/or follow an activity. Activities can be carried out during or after reading. Final outcomes can be individual or collaborative.

THE BOOK LISTS

There is a list of books on the back of each activity sheet. These aim to provide a starting point for busy teachers. Many of the titles will be familiar and you will have your own tried and tested favourites to add. The books are appropriate for group work but can also be used to encourage a greater range and variety in independent reading.

For guided group reading you will generally need multiples of some texts so that each child can have their own copy. Children in a group can then work on the same text using the same or different activities. At other times, a group could use the same activity with different texts.

The lists include lots of picture books, short novels and short stories because of their potential for teaching reading and their manageability in limited time. Children want to feel they are making progress with reading and can dismiss books that look too easy. Unfortunately, this means they can miss out on many excellent, multi-layered texts that have a lot to teach about reading.

Our lists will lead you to books that really earn their keep in the classroom. For maximum effectiveness in the development of reading, you must know both text and readers so that you can match them with the most appropriate activity. Most of the books we have suggested are in paperback and publishing details were correct when the lists were compiled.

The lists of books on the back of each activity are copyright and should not be photocopied.

How to create readers

The activities in *Reading Alive!* will work better and produce more positive results if children engage in the activities in a reader-friendly, literacy-rich environment. The following suggestions are designed to help you think about how you might adapt and sharpen the focus of what you already do. Often it's just a question of being more explicit. Some of these ideas could be planned into directed literacy time.

ESTABLISHING READING IDENTITY
☆ It's important to encourage children to become aware of themselves as readers. **Student View of Reading: Questionnaire** (page 57) is a good starting point in making 'reading chat' a feature of the classroom.
☆ Talk about your current reading (of whatever kind). Say why you are reading it, and what there is about it that you find challenging, boring, or impossible to put down. Encourage the children to do the same.
☆ Share ideas about favourite times and places to read.
☆ Be seen looking things up – from phone numbers to encyclopaedia references in books or on CD-ROM. Again, encourage children to do the same.
☆ Use the **Readership Award** (page 59) to make a statement about the kinds of reading you value in your classroom, for example: that quality of understanding is more important than number of books read.

THE READING ENVIRONMENT
☆ Think about the library, classroom and school as an environment for producing readers. Does the stock include materials of all kinds, including magazines, comics, newspapers, directories, maps, etc.?
☆ Is the stock well organised, attractive, in good condition, and current?
☆ How do the children learn to use and borrow reference material?
☆ Are there comfortable places to read or study?
☆ What do your displays say about reading and writing?
☆ Do you have a school bookshop, book club, book fair, book week, or other book events?
☆ Do you involve children in selecting books for the school, putting up displays and organising book events and related activities?

EXTENDING THE READING NETWORK
☆ Involve parents, friends and other interested volunteers with reading logs, shared reading, mentoring and family reading groups.
☆ Encourage them to help in the library and school bookshop, or with book events.
☆ Write to other readers, editors, authors and publishers about matters of interest and concern.

AVOIDING THINGS THAT KILL READING
Consider the following questions:
☆ Do you find yourself expressing negative attitudes through the way books are discussed, such as 'That's too hard/easy for you', 'Comics are for rainy dinner times', 'You've got to read a proper book now'?
☆ Is book talk limited to: 'Did you enjoy it?... Why?' (Often, that's an impossible question to answer.)
☆ Is opportunity for response limited to writing a book review?
☆ Do children have to write about every book they read?
☆ How often is the library used and what is it used for? Is there a teacher librarian with enough time to do the job enthusiastically?

☆ Are teachers too busy to keep up with what is being published for children, to read reviews and some of the books, and to talk to colleagues?
☆ How hard is it to keep your eyes on the real prize of creating readers in the fullest sense and avoid 'teaching to the test'.

INCREASING AWARENESS OF AUTHORS AND TITLES
☆ Build up an author clippings file and keep a file of author's birthdays.
☆ Pairs of readers could collaborate to create an author file.
☆ Have displays such as author or book 'of the month'.
☆ Compile a fiction database. Involve readers in deciding categories that will help them find the books they want to read, and in deciding which books fit into each category. Encourage them to keep the database up to date.
☆ Arrange an author visit with thorough preparation and follow-up.
☆ Compile a class 'Top Twenty' using suggestions from reading logs; encourage discussion and voting with cases for and against.
☆ Keep a file of authors' birthdays.

READING ALOUD AND BEING READ TO
☆ Make a habit of reading aloud different kinds of texts: jokes, riddles, items of interest from newspapers and magazines, reviews of books, films or television programmes, letters and postcards. Encourage children to contribute to this 'by-the-way' reading.
☆ Provide tapes of longer texts to help less confident readers sustain their focus on a story.
☆ Make time for reading promotional extracts, such as the blurbs on book covers.

READING LOGS AND RESPONSE JOURNALS
☆ Do you make the most of the records children keep of what they have read? Are these regularly reviewed with a teacher or other adult who will listen, learn, question? (*Did anything puzzle you as you were reading? Did it turn out as you expected?*). Share your own experience (*I read something like that*) and suggest ways forward (*You might like to try...*).
☆ Some of the *Reading Alive!* activities point the way towards keeping a full-scale response log or journal. Children could start by noting down their feelings, reactions, questions, predictions and personal connections at specified points or as they decide. These journals may be kept private or shared with the teacher or with other children who are reading the same book.

Reading Alive! and the National Literacy Strategy

This section is intended to help you decide how best to fit the *Reading Alive!* activities into your planning for literacy development. The lists that follow show how the activities in *Reading Alive!* can help with the attainment of the Key Stage 2 objectives, working at word, sentence and whole text level. The starting point each time is reading comprehension, but the natural interaction between reading and writing is developed by doing the activities. There are also opportunities for developing speaking and listening.

Numbers given in brackets indicate the year and term suggested in the DfEE's *Framework for Teaching* for focusing on a particular objective. You will see from this analysis how open the activities are. They can be used in any year, and you can build in differentiation with the texts you choose for your readers.

FRAMEWORK OBJECTIVES

ACTIVITIES: Listen to the Words on the Page (page 11); Word Magic (page 15)

☆ Explore words and phrases that describe settings or scenes; words and phrases that create impact – adjectives, powerful and expressive verbs; identifying words and phrases that support the child's view of a story or poem. **(3.1)**

☆ Collect examples of the style and voice of traditional story language; prepare extracts for reading aloud, focusing on expression, tone, volume, attention to punctuation and meaning. **(3.2)**

☆ Openings; how atmosphere is created; rhymes, distinctive rhythms, sound effects – alliteration, onomatopoeia; types of humour – word play, jokes. **(3.3)**

☆ How character and setting are built up from small details – reader response; verbs, adverbs. **(4.1)**

☆ Details which help to create imaginary worlds; words and phrases that create mood, arouse expectation, build tension, describe attitudes or emotions; figurative language in poetry or prose – similes; clues to when a text was written/set – usage, vocabulary, sentence structure; adjectives. **(4.2)**

☆ Poetic forms – couplets, stanza, rhyme, rhythm, alliteration, no rhyme; word order, use of connectives – conjunctions, adverbial phrases. **(4.3)**

☆ Story openings – impact on reader; analyse and compare poetic style – shades of meaning, effect of full rhyme, half-rhyme, internal rhyme; word play; word order. **(5.1)**

☆ Perform texts and extracts; poetic forms; literal and figurative language. **(5.2)**

☆ Language differences in older literature. **(5.3)**

☆ Articulate a personal response – how language affects the reader. **(6.1)**

☆ Structure of paragraphs; how writers use words – sound, rhythm, rhyme, assonance; figurative language – ambiguity, layers of meaning; word play – puns, nonsense words; creation of mood, feeling. **(6.2)**

☆ Style of individual writers – compare and contrast. **(6.3)**

ACTIVITIES: Alphabetical Authors (page 13); Booktails (page 17); Banquet of Reading (page 43); Country Couples (page 55)

☆ Readers support their views and identify specific words and phrases to support their viewpoint. **(3.1)**

☆ Be aware of authors, discuss preferences and give reasons for these. **(3.3)**

☆ Find out more about popular writers, poets – use this information to move on to more books. **(4.1)**

☆ Review a range of stories, identifying authors, themes, treatments; recognise how texts are targeted at particular readers. **(4.2)**

☆ Identify social, moral, cultural, issues in stories – provide evidence for this classification in the text; read more by a favourite writer – make comparisons and identify familiar features of that writer's work; describe and review reading habits – widen reading experience. **(4.3)**

☆ Discuss the enduring appeal of established authors; consider how a text can be rooted in the writer's experience. **(5.1)**

☆ Identify the features of different fiction genres – discuss their appeal. **(5.2)**

☆ Identify the point of view from which the story is told and how this affects the reader's response; explore the challenge and appeal of older literature. **(5.3)**

☆ Be familiar with the work of established authors, know what is special about their work, explain preferences in terms of authors' styles, themes; contribute to shared discussion about literature, responding to and building on the views of others. **(6.1)**

☆ Analyse the success of texts and writers in evoking responses in readers. **(6.2)**

☆ Write a brief synopsis of texts for back cover blurbs; compare and contrast the work of a single writer; look for and discuss connections and contrasts in the work of different writers. **(6.3)**

ACTIVITY: Teleletter (page 19)

☆ Identify typical story themes; plan main points structure; sequence key incidents. **(3.2)**

☆ Retell the main points of a story in sequence; refer to significant aspects of a text. **(3.3)**

☆ Explore chronology and narrative order; plan and sequence writing. **(4.1)**

☆ Identify the intended audience. **(4.2)**

☆ Evaluate a book with reference to specific aspects of the content and style. **(5.1)**

☆ Explore aspects of narrative structure; summarise texts in a specified number of words. **(6.1)**

☆ Write summaries relevant to purpose; write a brief synopsis, e.g. for a blurb. **(6.3)**

ACTIVITY: Detective Game (page 21)

☆ Discuss a range of story settings – words and phrases to describe the scene. **(3.1)**

☆ Consider typical story themes and structures; identify main characters; describe and sequence key incidents and episodes; main points structure. **(3.2)**

☆ Put main points in sequence. **(3.3)**

☆ Narrative order – introduction, build-ups, climaxes/conflicts, resolution. **(4.1)**

☆ Influence of setting on characters and events. **(4.2)**

☆ Structure of stories – sequence, complication, resolution; map texts in different ways showing developments and structure. **(5.1)**

☆ Use models to plan own writing; summarise a text in a specified number of words. **(6.1)**

☆ Narrative structures, story genres; parody. **(6.2)**

☆ Synopsis of texts. **(6.3)**

ACTIVITIES: Reading as Feeling (page 23); Reading is Feeling (page 41)

☆ Express own views about a story or poem – identify specific words and phrases. **(3.1)**

☆ Discuss behaviour of characters. **(3.2)**

☆ Discuss behaviour, feelings, and relationships of characters. **(3.3)**

☆ Reader response to how characters, settings and events are built up. **(4.1)**

☆ How language creates mood, expectations, tension, emotion. **(4.2)**

☆ Reader response to characters; develop reading – empathising, imaging. **(5.1)**

☆ Considering how language works on us. **(5.2)**

☆ Point of view and how this affects reader response. **(5.3)**

☆ Articulate a personal response – how and why a text affects a reader; contribute to shared discussion of texts. **(6.1)**

ACTIVITY: Predictions (page 25)

☆ Recognition and identification of the style and voice of different genres; identifying typical story themes and structures. **(3.2)**

☆ Refer to significant aspects of text – opening, build-up, atmosphere; distinguish between first and third person accounts. **(3.3)**

☆ Identify the main characteristics of key characters – use the information to predict actions; explore narrative order – introduction, conflict, resolution. **(4.1)**

☆ Understand how writers create imaginary worlds. **(4.2)**

☆ Identify characters' dilemmas, moral choices. **(4.3)**

☆ Develop an active attitude to reading – seeking answers, anticipating events; structure of different stories – complication and resolution. **(5.1)**

☆ Characteristic features of different fiction genres, myths, legends, fables. **(5.2)**

☆ Key features of different types of texts – stock characters, plot structures; how writers confirm, develop, undermine readers' expectations. **(6.2)**

ACTIVITIES: A letter to a book character (page 27); Identikits (page 35); Castaway Character (page 37); Goodies and Baddies (page 39); Zodiaction (page 47); Database Dating (page 51); Prunella Problem (page 49); This is Your Life (page 53)

☆ Express views about a story or poem. **(3.1)**

☆ Evaluate characters' behaviour and justify views; create portraits of characters in different media. **(3.2)**

☆ Distinguish characters' feelings, behaviour, relationships – refer to the text. **(3.3)**

☆ Investigate how characters are built up from small details and how the reader responds to them. **(4.1)**

☆ Understand how setting affects behaviour of characters. **(4.2)**

☆ Consider dilemmas faced by characters, identify problems and alternative courses of action, how characters behave, react, choose, the outcomes that result. **(4.3)**

☆ Readers' responses to characters (victims, heroes etc.); characters' relationships with other characters. **(5.1)**

☆ Author's treatment of different characters – minor characters, heroes, villains, different characters' perspectives on the action. **(5.2)**

☆ Identify point of view and how this affects response. **(5.3)**

☆ Articulate a personal response; contribute to shared discussion; consider how narrative viewpoint affects reader response. **(6.1)**

☆ Identify key features of different texts, e.g. stock characters. **(6.2)**

ACTIVITY: Emotion Trail (page 29)

☆ Identify plot structure, main characters; respond to and evaluate behaviour. **(3.2)**

☆ Retell the main points; consider the credibility of events; discuss and evaluate feelings, behaviour, relationships of characters. **(3.3)**

☆ Explore how characters are built up and how the reader responds; explore the chronology in the narrative, narrative order, climax, conflicts, resolution. **(4.1)**

☆ Dilemmas faced by characters – social, moral and cultural issues; how characters deal with them. **(4.3)**

☆ How characters are presented, how the reader responds; an active attitude to reading – empathy with and judgements on characters and events. **(5.1)**

☆ Narrative viewpoint, treatment of characters. **(5.2)**

☆ Point of view, impact on reader's response; consider and evaluate texts in relation to own experiences. **(5.3)**

☆ Take account of viewpoint and how it influences reader's view; articulate a personal response; identifying how a text affects the reader. **(6.1)**

ACTIVITY: Between the Lines and Behind the Lines (page 31)

☆ Become familiar with works by the same author. Be aware of authors. **(3.3)**
☆ Find out more about authors and poets. **(4.1)**
☆ Identify an author's themes and treatments; the idea of targeted/intended audiences. **(4.2)**
☆ Social, cultural, moral issues and dilemmas. **(4.3)**
☆ How texts can be rooted in the writer's experience; reader response and evaluation. (5.1)
☆ Distinguish between author and narrator. **(5.2)**
☆ Point of view – narrator, author. **(5.3)**
☆ Narrative viewpoint – influence on reader; personal response - how and why a text affects the reader. **(6.1)**
☆ To analyse how messages, moods, feelings and attitudes are conveyed. **(6.2)**

ACTIVITY: Taking the Temperature of a Book (page 33)

☆ Express views about a story or poem. **(3.1)**
☆ Consider credibility of events; response to characters. **(3.3)**
☆ Response to settings, characters, narrative order, build-up, climax/conflict, resolutions. **(4.1)**
☆ Writer's creation of an imaginary world; settings across a range of stories. **(4.2)**
☆ Issues and dilemmas. **(4.3)**
☆ Structure, pace, build-up, sequences, complications, resolutions; how characters are presented – through dialogue, action, description; active reading and evaluation; varied author appeal. **(5.1)**
☆ Narrative viewpoint; genre features; appeal of different texts. **(5.2)**
☆ Range of reading experience; response to point of view; challenge of older literature. **(5.3)**
☆ Articulate response; explain preferences in author style and themes; narrative viewpoint. **(6.1)**
☆ Narrative structure, handling of time; messages, moods, feelings, attitudes conveyed by writer; key features of different types of literary texts; author's success with readers. **(6.2)**

ACTIVITY: Bookburgers Reading Recipe (page 45)

☆ Story setting – words and phrases that describe scenes; presentation of dialogue. **(3.1)**
☆ Main and recurring characters. **(3.2)**
☆ How language creates atmosphere, tension; credibility of events; characters' feelings, behaviour, relationships. **(3.3)**
☆ Build up of settings and character – how reader responds; characteristics of main characters; narrative order and structure. **(4.1)**
☆ Creation and evocation of imaginary worlds; impact of setting on character and events; use of language to create mood, tension, arouse expectations, describe attitudes or emotions. **(4.2)**
☆ Explore dilemmas and issues in stories. **(4.3)**
☆ Structure of different stories – differences in pace, build-up, sequence, complication and resolution; presentation of characters – dialogue, action, description, relationships. **(5.1)**
☆ Features of different fiction genres. **(5.2)**
☆ Range of texts – different cultures; evaluate from own experience. **(5.3)**
☆ Articulate personal response; explain preferences in terms of author's style and themes; contribute to shared discussion. **(6.1)**
☆ Analyse the success of texts in evoking responses in the reader. **(6.2)**
☆ Describe and evaluate style. **(6.3)**

LISTEN TO THE WORDS ON THE PAGE !

and choose your favourite pieces for the empty balloons

The thought of talking to a stranger, even over the telephone, makes me feel like a mere limp lettuce leaf in the great salad of life.

MAHY, Margaret *Tingleberries, Tuckertubs and Telephones* (Puffin)

When the darkness crowds beyond the door, and the logs on the hearth burn clear red and fall in upon themselves, making caverns and ships and swords and dragons and strange faces in the heart of the fire, that is the time for story telling.

SUTCLIFF, Rosemary *The Road to Camlann* (Red Fox)

'What kind of pudding will you make?' Huey said. 'A wonderful pudding,' my father said. 'It will taste like a whole raft of lemons. It will taste like a night on the sea.'

CAMERON, Ann *The Julian Stories* (Yearling)

LISTEN TO THE WORDS ON THE PAGE

This activity helps readers and writers to focus on words, phrases, sentences and paragraphs. You can adapt the task to look at specific features of stories or poems, such as story openings, scene setting, the way mood is created or character established, rhyme, rhythm, figurative language and wordplay.

The books listed below have been chosen for the quality of the language and variety of voices. They include modern and traditional tales, myths, legends and folk tales, poetry and rhyme. When working with the picture books, readers will need to 'read' the pictures and think about the ways in which the words and pictures combine.

See also: **Word Magic**.

POETRY AND RHYME

AARDEMA, Vera *Bringing the Rain to Kapiti Plain* (Macmillan)
BERRY, James; NICHOLLS, Judith; NICHOLS, Grace; SCANNELL, Vernon; and SWEENEY, Matthew; ill. by
    Colin McNaughton *We Couldnt Provide Fish Thumbs* (Macmillan)
CAUSLEY, Charles; ill. by John Lawrence *Selected Poems for Children* (Macmillan)
HARRISON, Michael and STUART-CLARK, Christopher *Oxford Book of Story Poems* (Oxford)
HOBAN, Russell; ill. by Patrick Benson *The Last of the Wallendas and Other Poems* (Hodder)
HARRISON, Michael and STUART-CLARK, Christopher (eds) *The Oxford Book of Story Poems* (Oxford)
NICHOLS, Grace *Give Yourself a Hug* (Puffin)
NOYES, Alfred and KEEPING, Charles *The Highwayman* (Oxford)
PATTEN, Brian (ed.) *The Puffin Book of Twentieth Century Verse* (Puffin)
STEWART, Pauline *Singing Down the Breadfruit* (Red Fox)
WATERS, Fiona (ed.) *The Poetry book* (Dolphin)
WILSON, Raymond (ed.) *The Puffin book of classic verse* (Puffin)

STORIES

AIKEN, Joan; ill. by Jan Pienkowski *A Necklace of Raindrops* (Puffin)
AIKEN, Joan *Fog Hounds, Wind Cat, Sea Mice* (Hodder)
AIKEN, Joan; ill. by Quentin Blake *The Winter Sleepwalker* (Red Fox)
CAMERON, Ann *The Julian Stories* and series (Yearling)
GARFIELD, Leon *Shakespeare Stories* (Puffin)
GARNER, Alan *Bag of Moonshine* (Collins)
HUGHES, Ted *How the Whale Became and Other Stories* (Faber)
HUGHES, Ted *The Dream Fighter and other Creation tales* (Faber)
JAFFREY, Madhur and FOREMAN, Michael *Seasons of Splendour* (Puffin)
JONES, Terry *Fairy Tales* (Puffin)
KIPLING, Rudyard *Just-so Stories* (several publishers)
LOBEL, Arnold *Frog and Toad are Friends* and series (Mammoth)
MAHY, Margaret *Jam: A True story* (Puffin)
MAHY, Margaret *Tingleberries, Tuckertubs and telephones* (Puffin)
SUTCLIFF, Rosemary *Beowulf* (Red Fox)
SUTCLIFF, Rosemary *Dragon Slayer* (Red Fox)
SUTCLIFF, Rosemary *The High Deeds of Finn McCool* (Red Fox)
SUTCLIFF, Rosemary *The Road to Camlann* (Red Fox)
WILLIAMSON, Duncan *Fireside Tales of the Traveller Children* (Canongate)
WOLFSON, Margaret Olivia *Marriage of the Rain Goddess* (Barefoot Books)

ALPHABETICAL AUTHORS

NAME _____

Every time you read a book, fill in the author's surname in the correct alphabetical book. Can you find any authors for Z?

A
AHLBERG, Janet and Allan
AIKEN, Joan
AMBRUS, Victor
ANNO, Mitsumasa
ASHLEY, Bernard

A

B

C

D

E

F

G

H

I

J

K

L

M

N

O

P

Q

R

S

T

U

V

W

X

Y

Z

MY FAVOURITE AUTHOR IN _____ WAS:
_{YEAR}

_____

© 1999 A&C Black (Publishers) Ltd. This page may be copied for classroom use.

13

ALPHABETICAL AUTHORS

This activity will especially appeal to the collectors and list compilers in the class. It makes a good foundation for building author recognition, assembling information about authors, writing letters and creating author displays. The following list suggests some names to get you started.

See also: **Booktails, Banquet of Reading, Country Couples.**

A
AARDEMA, Vera
AHLBERG, Janet & Allan
AIKEN, Joan
ANNO, Mitsumasa
ASHLEY, Bernard
AVERY, Gillian

B
BANKS, Lynne Reid
BAWDEN, Nina
BLACKMAN, Marjorie
BLAKE, Quentin
BLUME, Judy
BROWN, Jeff
BROWNE, Anthony
BURNINGHAM, John
BYARS, Betsy

C
CAUSLEY, Charles
CAMERON, Ann
CHAMBERS, Aidan
CLEARY, Beverley
COLE, Babette
CRESSWELL, Helen
CROSS, Gillian

D
DAHL, Roald
DAVIES, Andrew
De JONG, Meindert
DODD, Lynley
DOHERTY, Berlie
DUPASQUIER, Philippe

E
EDWARDS, Dorothy

F
FARMER, Penelope
FINE, Ann
FOREMAN, Michael
FRENCH, Fiona

G
GARDAM, Jane
GARFIELD, Leon
GARNER, Alan
GAVIN, Jamila
GERAS, Adele
GODDEN, Rumer
GOSCINNY, Rene
GRAHAM, Bob

H
HEIDE, Florence Parry
HENDRY, Diana
HINTON, Nigel
HOBAN, Russell
HOWKER, Janni
HUGHES, Shirley
HUGHES, Ted
HUTCHINS, Pat

I
IMPEY, Rosel
IRESON, Barbara

J
JANSSON, Tove
JONES, Terry
JUNGMAN, Ann

K
KAYE, Geraldine
KEMP, Gene
KERR, Judith
KING, Clive
KING-SMITH, Dick
KLEIN, Robin

L
LAVELLE, Sheila
LEESON, Robert
LEWIS, C.S.
LINDGREN, Astrid
LINGARD, Joan
LIVELY, Penelope
LOBEL, Arnold
LOWRY, Lois

M
McCAUGHREAN, Geraldine
McGOUGH, Roger
McKEE, David
MAHY, Margaret
MARK, Jan
MARSHALL, James
MAYNE, William
MORGAN, Alison
MORPURGO, Michael
MURPHY, Jill

N
NAIDOO, Beverley
NEEDLE, Jan
NICHOLS, Grace
NIMMO, Jenny

O
OAKLEY, Graham
OBRIEN, Robert
ORAM, Hiawyn
OXENBURY, Helen

P
PARK, Ruth
PATERSON, Katherine
PEARCE, Philippa
PILLING, Ann
POWLING, Chris
PRICE, Susan

R
RAYNER, Mary
ROCKWELL, Thomas
RODDA, Emily
RODGERS, Mary
ROSEN, Michael
ROSS, Tony
ROWLING, J.K.

S
SCIESZKA, Jon
SENDAK, Maurice
STEIG, William
STEVENSON, James
STORR, Catherine
STRONG, Jeremy
SUTCLIFF, Rosemary
SWINDELLS, Robert

T
TOMLINSON, Jill
TOWNSON, Hazel
TROUGHTON, Joanna

U
UDERZO, Albert
UNGERER, Tomi
URE, Jean
UTTLEY, Alison

V
VAN ALLSBERG, Chris
VIORST, Judith

W
WADDELL, Martin
WALSH, Jill Paton
WELLS, Rosemary
WESTALL, Robert
WHITE, E.B.
WILLIAMS, Ursula Moray
WILSON, Bob
WILSON, Jacqueline

Y
YEOMAN, John

Z
ZIEFERT, Harriet
ZION, Gene
ZOLOTOW, Charlotte

word magic

Words you love to say softly, slowly, fast, loudly, silently, words you like to write, words you like to see, words . . .

Pugilistical
AHLBERG, Janet and Allan *Please Mrs Butler* (Puffin)

Pulverized
MAHY, Margaret *The Great Piratical Rumbustification* (Puffin)

Diddling
HOBAN, Russell *Dinner at Alberta's* (Puffin)

MAGIC WORD LIST

_____

Pugilistical
_____

Pulverized
_____

Diddling
_____

_____

_____

_____

_____

_____

_____

_____

Swap your list with friends What were their words? Where did they come from?

WORD MAGIC

Word Magic can be used to explore and enjoy rich, imaginative and unusual language. It can also focus attention on the origins of words, their sounds and the associations we have with them.

You may want to start by working with extracts you have selected. Discuss interesting or unusual words with the class or group, and try out ways of reading them aloud. Once the children have the idea (and a dictionary) they can go it alone.

POETRY

AGARD, John; COPE, Wendy; McGOUGH, Roger; MITCHELL, Adrian; PATTEN, Brian
     Another day in your foot and I would have died (Macmillan)
AHLBERG, Allan *Please Mrs Butler* (Puffin)
BERRY, James; ill. by BRIERLEY, Louise *Celebration Song* (Puffin)
CORBETT, Pie (ed.) *It's raining cats and dogs* (Puffin)
ELIOT, T.S. *Old Possum's Book of Practical Cats* (Faber)
LEAR, Edward; ill. by OXENBURY, Helen *The Quangle Wangle's Hat* (Mammoth)
McGOUGH, Roger *Bad, Bad Cats* (Puffin)
McGOUGH, Roger *Sky in the Pie* (Puffin)
PLATH, Sylvia *The Bed Book* (Faber)
ROSEN, Michael *Hairy Tales and Nursery Crimes* (Collins)
ROSEN, Michael *Spollyollydiddlytiddlyitis* (Walker)
ROSEN, Michael *You Wait Till I'm Older* (Puffin)
ROSEN, Michael (ed.) *Walking the Bridge of Your Nose* (Kingfisher)
STEWART, Pauline *Singing Down the Breadfruit* (Red Fox)

STORIES

AHLBERG, Allan and Janet *The Clothes Horse and Other Stories* (Puffin)
GARNER, Alan *The Stone Book Quartet* (Collins)
HOBAN, Russell *Dinner at Alberta's* (Puffin)
HOBAN, Russell; ill. by BLAKE, Quentin *How Tom Beat Captain Najork and
     His Hired Sportsmen* (Red Fox)
HOBAN, Russell; ill. by BLAKE, Quentin *A Near Thing for Captain Najork* (Red Fox)
HUTCHINS, Pat *Don't Forget the Bacon* (Picture Puffin)
JANSSON, Tove *Finn Family Moomintroll* [and series] (Puffin)
JUSTER, Norton *The Phantom Tollbooth* (Collins)
KIPLING, Rudyard *Just-so Stories* (several publishers)
KORALEK, Jenny; ill. by MAYHEW, James *The Boy and the Cloth of Dreams* (Walker)
MAHY, Margaret *The Pirate's Mixed-up Voyage* (Puffin)
MAHY, Margaret *The Chewing-gum Rescue* (Puffin)
MAHY, Margaret *The Great Piratical Rumbustification* (Puffin)

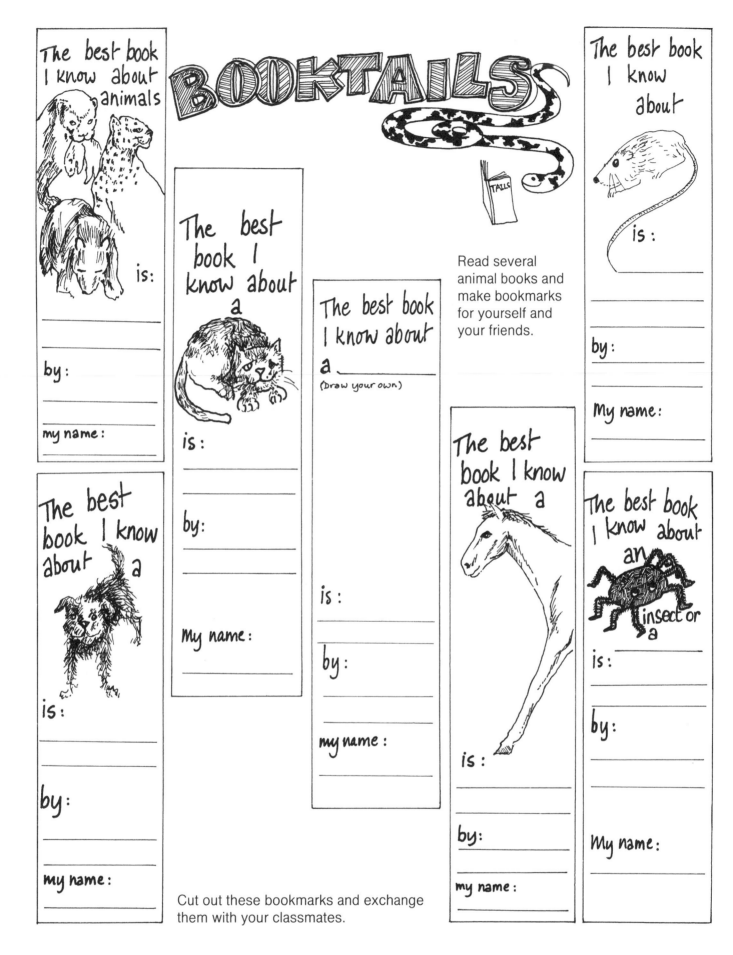

BOOKTAILS

The best book I know about animals is:

_____

by:

_____

my name:

_____

The best book I know about a [cat] is:

_____

by:

_____

My name:

_____

The best book I know about a _____ (Draw your own) is:

_____

by:

_____

my name:

_____

Read several animal books and make bookmarks for yourself and your friends.

The best book I know about _____ is:

_____

by:

_____

My name:

_____

The best book I know about a [dog] is:

_____

by:

_____

my name:

_____

The best book I know about a [horse] is:

_____

by:

_____

my name:

_____

The best book I know about an insect or a [spider] is:

_____

by:

_____

My name:

_____

Cut out these bookmarks and exchange them with your classmates.

BOOKTAILS

This activity is designed to create lively discussion about books and to promote reading as an enjoyable thing to do. The activity focuses on animal stories but you could use it as a model and change the theme to suit the reading preferences and needs of your class. You might like to encourage the children to design their own bookmarks. It can circulate between friends, be attached to books or be displayed. Those which attract general approval could be backed and laminated to prolong life.

See also: **Alphabetical Authors, Banquet of Reading, Country Couples, Teleletter.**

CATS

ARKLE, Phyllis *The Railway Cat* series (Hodder)
ASHLEY, Bernard *Calling for Sam* from the *Clipper Street* stories (Orchard)
ASHTON, Jay *Keeping Cats* (Oxford)
BROWN, Ruth *Our Cat Flossie* (Red Fox)
CASTOR, Harriet *Fat Puss* stories (Puffin)
HATHORN, Libby and ROGERS, Gregory *Way Home* (Red Fox)
HOOKE, Nina Warner *The Snow Kitten* (Puffin)
LONG, Jonathan and PAUL, Korky *The Cat that Scratched* (Red Fox)
PEARCE, Philippa *Mrs Cockle's Cat* (Puffin)

DOGS

CLARKE, Gus *Scratch 'n' Sniff* (Andersen)
De JONG, Meindert *Hurry Home Candy* (Collins)
KEMP, Gene *Dog's Journey* (Collins)
KING-SMITH, Dick *Yob* from the *Banana* series (Heinemann)
KING-SMITH, Dick *The Invisible Dog* (Puffin)
LEESON, Robert *The Dog Who Changed the World* (Puffin)
LONG, Jonathan and PAUL, Korky *The Dog that Dug* (Red Fox)
NEWBERY, Linda *Whistling Jack* (Collins)
WELLS, Rosemary (retelling); ill. by JEFFERS, Susan *Lassie Come Home* (Puffin)

MICE, HAMSTERS, GERBILS

BANKS, Lynne Reid *I Houdini* (Collins)
CORBETT, W.J. *Pentecost* series (Mammoth)
OAKLEY, Graham *The Church Mice* series (Macmillan)
OBRIEN, Robert *Mrs Frisby and the Rats of NIMH* (Puffin)
PEARCE, Philippa *The Battle of Bubble and Squeak* (Puffin)
KING-SMITH, Dick *The Terrible Trins* (Puffin)

HORSES

COOKSON, Catherine *The Nipper* (Corgi)
FIDLER, Kathleen *Haki, the Shetland Pony* (Canongate)
GARDAM, Jane *Kit Stories* (Walker)
PEYTON, K.M. and CHEPLAR, Anna *The Pony that Went to Sea* (Mammoth)

OTHER ANIMALS

BAWDEN, Nina *Keeping Henry* (Puffin)
BANKS, Lynne Reid *Harry the Poisonous Centipede* (Collins)
BURNFORD, Sheila *The Incredible Journey* (Hodder)
BYARS, Betsy *The Midnight Fox* (Puffin)
CHAMBERS, Aidan *Seal Secret* (Red Fox)
CHARLES, Faustin *Once Upon an Animal* (Bloomsbury) [poetry]
CURRY, Jennifer *Hands Off Our Hens* (Young Hippo, Animals)
DANN, Colin *Animals of Farthing Wood* series (Red Fox)
DERWENT, Lavinia *Sula* (Canongate)
DOHERTY, Berlie *Willa and Old Miss Anna* (Walker) [Three stories]
HERRIOT, James Vet stories in picture book versions, various illustrators (Macmillan)
KEMP, Gene *Tamworth Pig* series (Faber)
KEMP, Gene *Dog's Journey: a Goosey Farm Story* (Collins)
MORGAN, Alison *Christabel* (Walker)
MORPURGO, Michael *Why the Whales Came* (Mammoth)
MORPURGO, Michael (ed.) *Muck and Magic Stories from the Countryside* (Mammoth)
NICHOLS, Grace *Asana and the Animals* (Walker) [poetry]

teleletter

BREVITY IS THE SOUL OF WIT... AND SELLING

Choose a book with plenty of action. Take one really exciting incident and tell a friend about it in a TELELETTER. Say just enough about the plot to make your friend really want to read the book. Do not use more than 30 words. Here is an example:

Three children in a stranger's camper van [Stop]
One sees more than he should [Stop]
They know too much [Stop]
They are kidnapped and in danger [Stop]
(*Hideaway* by Ruth Thomas)

Fold the TELELETTER in three and write your friend's name on the outside.

WRITE NAME OF FRIEND ON BACK WHEN YOU HAVE FOLDED IT...

AUTHOR _____

TITLE _____

(A) (FOLD (A) SO THAT TIP OF ENVELOPE SLIDES INTO SLOT

_____

_____

_____

_____

_____

WORD COUNT____ (DO NOT COUNT 'STOP')   (MAXIMUM 30 WORDS)

(B) ·

FROM: _____

CUT HERE   SLOT

(C) (FOLD ALONG (B) SO THAT (C) MEETS (A))

TELELETTER

This challenging activity encourages children to think through the difficult process of identifying the essential features of a story and eliminating details in the retelling. It can help to develop ideas about themes, genres and narrative structure – especially critical incidents, problems and conflicts. The children also need to decide how much of the story to reveal and how to tempt their friend to read the book.

Teleletters can circulate between children in the class and be displayed to promote reading and help selection. This activity is particularly well-suited to collaborative work in groups or pairs.

AHLBERG, Allan and Janet *Burglar Bill* (Mammoth)
AHLBERG, Allan and Janet *The Vanishment of Thomas Tull* (Puffin)
AIKEN, Joan *The Wolves of Willoughby Chase* and series (Red Fox)
ASHLEY, Bernard *Justin and the Demon Drop Kick* (Puffin)
BLACKMAN, Marjorie *A.N.T.I.D.O.T.E.* (Corgi)
BROWN, Jeff *Flat Stanley* (Mammoth)
BYARS, Betsy *The Eighteenth Emergency* (Red Fox)
CHAMBERS, Aidan *The Present Takers* (Red Fox)
COOPER, Susan *Over Sea, Under Stone* and series (Puffin)
CROSS, Gillian *The Demon Headmaster* and series (Puffin)
DAHL, Roald *Fantastic Mr Fox* (Puffin)
DAHL, Roald *The BFG* (Puffin)
DAVIES, Andrew *Conrad's War* (Scholastic)
DAVIES, Hunter *Flossie Teacake* series (Red Fox)
FINE, Anne *The Chicken Gave It To Me* (Mammoth)
GARFIELD, Leon *The Stolen Watch* (Puffin)
HEIDE, Florence Parry *The Shrinking of Treehorn* (Puffin)
HINTON, Nigel *Beaver Towers* (Puffin)
HUGHES, Shirley *Chips and Jessie* (Red Fox)
LEESON, Robert *Tom's Private War* (Puffin)
NORRISS, Andrew *Aquila* (Puffin)
OBRIEN, Robert *Mrs Frisby and the Rats of NIMH* (Puffin)
PILLING, Ann *Henry's Leg* (Puffin)
PILLING, Ann *Mother's Daily Scream* (Puffin)
ROWLING, J.K. *Harry Potter and the Philosopher's Stone* (Bloomsbury)
SWINDELLS, Robert *Voyage to Valhalla* (Hodder)
SWINDELLS, Robert *Hurricane Summer* (Mammoth)
THOMAS, Ruth *Hideaway* (Red Fox)
WALSH, Jill Paton *Gaffer Samson's Luck* (Puffin)
WILSON, Bob *Stanley Bagshaw and the Twenty-two Ton Whale* and series (Puffin)
WILSON, Jacqueline *Cliffhanger* (Yearling)

PLOT ?
MOTIVE ?
STYLE ?

NAME OF DETECTIVE _____

Read a book with plenty of action and write it up as a detective's case study.

AUTHOR _____ TITLE _____

DETECTIVE GAME

CASE STUDY

WHO? (The protagonists, main characters, villains, victims, heroines, heroes)

_____
_____
_____
_____

WHAT happened? To whom? WHEN? HOW?

_____
_____
_____
_____
_____
_____

WHERE? Place ; location ; country ? Did it have any influence on what happened ?

_____
_____

WHY? For what reason? Motives? Causes? Explanations? Evidence? Factors?

_____
_____
_____

So? With what result? Conclusion? What happened in the end? OK?

_____
_____
_____

DETECTIVE GAME

This activity provides a framework for considering narrative structure and the language we need for talking about it. You can also use *Detective Game* to introduce words such as conflict, climax and resolution.

AHLBERG, Allan *Woof!* (Puffin)
AHLBERG, Allan *It Was a Dark and Stormy Night* (Puffin)
ALCOCK, Vivien *The Face at the Window* (Mammoth)
BANKS, Lynne Reid *Indian in the Cupboard* (Collins)
BAWDEN, Nina *The Finding* (Puffin)
BLACKMAN, Marjorie *A.N.T.I.D.O.T.E.* (Corgi)
BLAKE, Quentin *Clown* (Red Fox) [a wordless picture book]
CHESHIRE, Simon *Jeremy Brown of the Secret Service* (Walker)
CORBETT, W.J. *The Battle of Chinnbrook Wood* (Hodder)
CROSS, Gillian *The Great Elephant Chase* (Puffin)
DAVIES, Andrew *Conrad's War* (Scholastic)
GARFIELD, Leon *Fair's Fair* (Walker)
GARFIELD, Leon *The Apprentices* (Mammoth)
HENDRY, Diana *Harvey Angell* (Red Fox)
HUGHES, Shirley *It's Too Frightening For Me* (Puffin)
HUTCHINS, Pat *The Mona Lisa Mystery* (Red Fox)
KING-SMITH, Dick *The Fox Busters* (Puffin)
LEESON, Robert *Tom's Private War* (Puffin)
NAIDOO, Beverley *No Turning Back* (Puffin)
NORRISS, Andrew *Aquila* (Puffin)
MORPURGO, Michael *King of the Cloud Forests* (Mammoth)
PILLING, Ann *Mother's Daily Scream* (Puffin)
PULLMAN, Philip *New Cut Gang* series (Puffin)
THOMAS, Ruth *The Runaways* (Red Fox)
TOWNSON, Hazel *Charlie's Champion Chase* and other *Charlie* titles (Mammoth)
WAUGH, Sylvia *The Mennyms* and sequel (Red Fox)
WESTALL, Robert *Blitz* (Collins) [four stories]

YOUR NAME: _____

AUTHOR: _____

TITLE: _____

DEPRESSED HOLLOW CURIOUS CONTENTED BETRAYED DISGUSTED ANXIOUS
VULNERABLE INTRIGUED OVERJOYED CONFUSED UPSET BAFFLED BITTER
ELATED FULFILLED PROUD HAPPY DELIGHTED AMUSED WILD
DISMAYED INVOLVED SAD BEWILDERED RELIEVED DISAPPOINTED
SATISFIED DEJECTED CROSS
DISTRESSED ANGRY DETACHED
ANGUISHED CALM FURIOUS
DEFENCELESS PLEASED ALONE
DISPIRITED HURT SCEPTICAL DISTRAUGHT INDIGNANT MAD LONELY

READING AS FEELING

When you've read your book, think about what you felt

I felt .... when ....

....

....

I felt .... when ....

....

....

I felt .... when ....

....

....

I felt .... when ....

....

....

I felt .... when ....

....

....

READING AS FEELING

Reading and Feeling helps young readers to reflect upon their response to a book and to articulate their thoughts. It can be the first step towards keeping a response log or journal.

The faces have ambiguous expressions to indicate that our responses as readers are rarely as obvious as 'happy' or 'sad'. Teachers can help readers discover a wonderful range of feeling words. Your knowledge of the needs and capabilities of the readers in your class will enable you to decide how much to intervene and whether to encourage reading responses at stages during the reading rather than at the end. When children are used to recording their responses in this way, the activity can be used by groups working independently of the teacher.

See also: **Reading is Feeling**.

STORIES

ASHLEY, Bernard *Taller Than Before* (Orchard)
ASHLEY, Bernard *Dinner Ladies Don't Count* (Puffin)
BAWDEN, Nina *The Peppermint Pig* (Puffin)
BLUME, Judy *Freckle Juice* (Macmillan)
BLUME, Judy *Superfudge* (Macmillan)
BLUME, Judy *Fudge-a-mania* (Macmillan)
BLUME, Judy *Tales of a Fourth Grade Nothing* (Macmillan)
BYARS, Betsy *The Cybil War* (Red Fox)
CHAMBERS, Aidan *Seal Secret* (Red Fox)
CHAMBERS, Aidan *The Present Takers* (Red Fox)
CROSS, Gillian *The Mintyglo Kid* and other Barney, Spag and Clipper stories (Mammoth)
FARMER, Penelope *Saturday by Seven* (Walker)
FINE, Anne *Bill's New Frock* (Mammoth)
GARDAM, Jane *Kit Stories* (Walker)
GARDAM, Jane *A Few Fair Days* (Walker)
GODDEN, Rumer *The Story of Holly and Ivy* (Puffin)
HOOKE, Nina Warner *The Snow Kitten* (Puffin)
KAYE, Geraldine *Comfort Herself* (Scholastic)
LINGARD, Joan *The Twelfth Day of July* (Puffin)
MAGORIAN, Michelle *Goodnight Mr Tom* (Puffin)
MORPURGO, Michael *The Marble Crusher* (Mammoth) [three stories]
RAYNER, Mary *The Small Good Wolf* (Mammoth)
TOMLINSON, Jill *The Owl Who Was Afraid of the Dark* (Puffin)

PICTURE BOOKS

BLAKE, Quentin *Clown* (Red Fox)
BROWNE, Anthony *Gorilla* (Walker)
HUGHES, Shirley *Dogger* (Red Fox)
ORAM, Hiawyn and KITAMURA, Satoshi *Angry Arthur* (Red Fox)
ORAM, Hiawyn and KITAMURA, Satoshi *In the Attic* (Red Fox)
OWEN, Paul *Storm Boy* (Barefoot Books)
SENDAK, Maurice *Where the Wild Things Are* (Collins)
WAGNER, Jenny and BROOKS, Ron *John Brown, Rose and the Midnight Cat* (Puffin)

PREDICTIONS : PREDICTIONS

YOUR NAME: _____

AUTHOR: _____

TITLE: _____

READ THE FIRST CHAPTER, THEN STOP!

What do you think is going to happen? _____
_____
_____

Who are the main characters? _____
_____

What are they like? _____
_____
_____
_____

Do you feel caught up with the story and characters already?   Why?   Why not?
_____
_____
_____

Is there a main problem in the story . . . something the main character is going to have to overcome/come to grips with? How will he/she do it? _____
_____
_____
_____
_____

NOW FINISH THE BOOK

Were your predictions right?   Why/How? _____
_____
_____
_____
_____
_____
_____
_____

PREDICTIONS

It can be difficult getting into a book, especially one that offers new reading experiences and challenges. *Predictions* supports children as they learn some of the basic strategies that experienced readers use when they encounter first chapters. It can also help in the lead up towards the keeping of a response log or journal.

AHLBERG, Allan *The Better Brown Stories* (Puffin)
AIKEN, Joan *Cold Shoulder Road* (Red Fox)
ASHLEY, Bernard *Dinner Ladies Don't Count* (Puffin)
BANKS, Lynne Reid *The Indian in the Cupboard* [and sequel] (Collins)
CRESSWELL, Helen *The Sea Piper* (Hodder)
DOHERTY, Berlie *Daughter of the Sea* (Puffin)
FARMER, Penelope *Saturday by Seven* (Walker)
FINE, Anne *The Granny Project* (Mammoth)
FINE, Anne *Flour Babies* (Puffin)
GARFIELD, Leon *Fair's Fair* (Walker)
GARFIELD, Leon *Smith* (Puffin)
GAVIN, Jamila *Someone's Watching, Someone's Waiting* (Mammoth)
HINTON, Nigel *Beaver Towers* (Puffin)
JENNINGS, Paul *The Paw Thing* (Puffin)
KING-SMITH, Dick *Saddlebottom* and other titles (Puffin)
LEESON, Robert *Never Kiss Frogs* (Puffin)
LIVELY, Penelope *The Ghost of Thomas Kempe* (Puffin)
MORPURGO, Michael *The Wreck of the Zanzibar* (Mammoth)
NIMMO, Jenny *Seth and the Strangers* (Mammoth)
NIMMO, Jenny *Griffin's Castle* (Mammoth)
RAYNER, Mary *The Small Good Wolf* (Mammoth)
RODGERS, Mary *Freaky Friday* (Puffin)
SWINDELLS, Robert *The Ice Palace* (Puffin)
SWINDELLS, Robert *World Eater* (Yearling)
THOMAS, Ruth *The Class That Went Wild* (Red Fox)
THOMAS, Ruth *The Runaways* (Red Fox)
WALSH, Jill Paton *Thomas and the Tinners* (Macdonald)
WILSON, Jacqueline *Double Act* (Yearling)

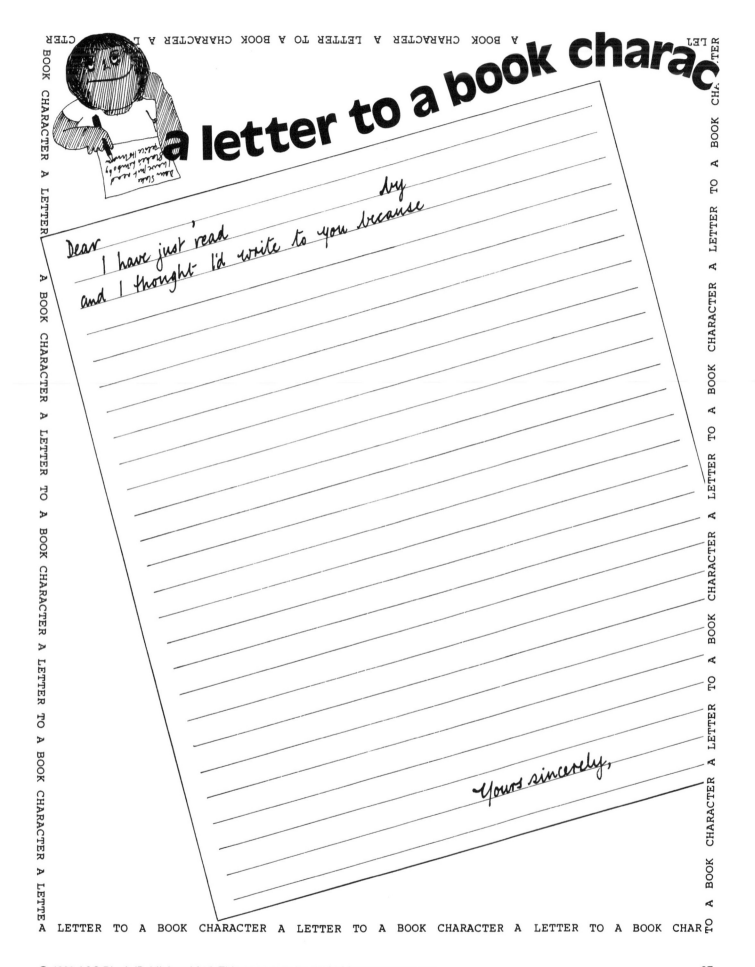

a letter to a book charac

Dear   I have just read   for
and I thought I'd write to you because

Yours sincerely,

A LETTER TO A BOOK CHARACTER

This activity works best when readers have connected strongly with the world of a book. It encourages them to consider issues and think about the perspectives of different characters. It encourages empathy with behaviour and events, understanding of motivation, and evaluation of behaviour and outcomes. This could also be a useful prelude to 'hot-seating' and other drama-based innovations.

See also: **Identikits, Castaway Characters, Goodies and Baddies, Zodiaction, Database Dating, Prunella Problem, This is Your Life.**

STORIES

BAWDEN, Nina *Carrie's War* (Puffin)
BLUME, Judy *Tales of a Fourth Grade Nothing* (Macmillan)
BLUME, Judy *Otherwise known as Sheila the Great* (Macmillan)
BYARS, Betsy *The Midnight Fox* (Red Fox)
CHAMBERS, Aidan *Seal Secret* (Red Fox)
CROSS, Gillian *The Mintyglo Kid* (Mammoth)
CROSS, Gillian *Gobbo the Great* (Mammoth)
CROSS, Gillian *Swimathon* (Mammoth)
CROSS, Gillian *Save our School* (Mammoth)
DOHERTY, Berlie *Tilly Mint and the Dodo* (Mammoth)
FITZHUGH, Louise *Harriet the Spy* (Puffin)
GEORGE, Jean Craighead *Julie of the Wolves* (Red Fox)
JARMAN, Julia *More Jessame Stories* (Mammoth)
KERR, Judith *When Hitler Stole Pink Rabbit* (Collins)
KERR, Judith *Out of the Hitler Time* (Collins)
LOWRY, Lois *Anastasia Krupnik* series (Collins)
MAGORIAN, Michelle *Goodnight Mr Tom* (Puffin)
MARK, Jan *The Dead Letter Box* (Puffin)
MORPURGO, Michael *The Marble Crusher* (Mammoth)
PARK, Ruth *Playing Beatie Bow* (Puffin)
PATERSON, Katherine *A Bridge to Terabithia* (Puffin)
SELWAY, Martina *Wish You Were Here* (Red Fox)
SELWAY, Martina *I Hate Roland Roberts* (Red Fox)
WALSH, Jill Paton *Gaffer Samson's Luck* (Puffin)
WILSON, Jacqueline *The Suitcase Kid* (Yearling)
WILSON, Jacqueline *Double Act* (Yearling)

PICTURE BOOKS

BROWNE, Anthony *Piggybook* (Walker)
BURNINGHAM, John *Where's Julius?* (Red Fox)
DUPASQUIER, Philippe *Dear Daddy* (Puffin)
HOFFMAN, Mary and BINCH, Caroline *Amazing Grace* and other titles (Frances Lincoln)
FLOURNEY, Valerie and PINKNEY, Jerry *The Patchwork Quilt* (Puffin)
HEIDE, Florence Parry and GILLILAND, Judith Heide; ill. by Ted Lewin *The Day of Ahmed's Secret* (Gollancz)
JAMES, Simon *Dear Greenpeace* (Walker)
WADDELL, Martin and DUPASQUIER, Philippe *Going West* (Puffin)

emotion trail

YOUR NAME: _____

AUTHOR: _____

TITLE: _____

When you have read your book, work out the main events in the story (the plot) for Column 1, what the main character felt like during these events (the emotional plot) for Column 2, and what **you** felt like for Column 3.

1 PLOT (WHAT HAPPENED)	2 MAIN CHARACTER: HOW SHE/HE FELT	3 WHAT YOU FELT LIKE READING ABOUT IT

Did this book say anything to you about your own life and emotions? Your family? Your friends? Your own character and personality?

EMOTION TRAIL

Emotion Trail is another good way to start working towards a full response journal. The activity provides a structure for groups or pairs to talk about their responses to a text and explore narrative structure. These shared responses provide a valuable basis for recording individual response.

STORIES

ASHLEY, Bernard *Dinner Ladies Don't Count* (Puffin)
ASHLEY, Bernard *Taller than Before* (Orchard)
ASHLEY, Chris *Wasim in the Deep End* (Red Fox)
BRANFORD, Henrietta *Fire, Bed, Bone* (Walker)
CHAMBERS, Aidan *The Present Takers* (Red Fox)
CRESSWELL, Helen *A Gift from Winklesea* (Hodder)
CRESSWELL, Helen *Mystery at Winklesea* (Hodder)
CROSS, Gillian *The Great Elephant Chase* (Puffin)
FINE, Anne *Madame Doubtfire* (Puffin)
GARDAM, Jane *Kit Stories* (Walker)
GAVIN, Jamila *Someone's Watching, Someone's Waiting* (Mammoth)
HOWKER, Janni *Badger on the Barge* (Walker) [short stories]
LIVELY, Penelope *Fanny and the Monsters* (Mammoth)
LOVEDAY, John *Goodbye Buffalo Sky* (Bloomsbury)
MAHY, Margaret *The Five Sisters* (Puffin)
McCAUGHREAN, Geraldine *The Wooden Horse* (Orchard Myths)
McCAUGHREAN, Geraldine *Pandora's Box* (Orchard Myths)
MORPURGO, Michael *The Dancing Bear* (Collins)
NEWBERY, Linda *Whistling Jack* (Collins)
NIMMO, Jenny *The Owl Tree* (Walker)
PEARCE, Philippa *A Dog So Small* (Puffin)
PEARCE, Philippa *What the Neighbours Did* (Puffin) [short stories]
PEARCE, Philippa *Tom's Midnight Garden* (Puffin)
PILLING, Ann *Mother's Daily Scream* (Puffin)
SMITH, Alexander McCall *The Perfect Hamburger* (Puffin)
SUTCLIFF, Rosemary *Beowulf: Dragon Slayer* (Puffin)
SWINDELLS, Robert *World Eater* (Yearling)
SWINDELLS, Robert *Jacqueline Hyde* (Yearling)
WILSON, Jacqueline *The Bed and Breakfast Star* (Yearling)
WILSON, Jacqueline *Cliffhanger* (Yearling)

PICTURE BOOKS

BLAKE, Quentin *Clown* (Red Fox)
BLAKE, Quentin *The Story of the Dancing Frog* (Red Fox)
BROWNE, Anthony *The Tunnel* (Walker)
BURNINGHAM, John *Granpa* (Red Fox)
WADDELL, Martin and DUPASQUIER, Philippe *Going West* (Puffin)
WAGNER, Jenny and BROOKS, Ron *John Brown, Rose and the Midnight Cat* (Puffin)

YOUR NAME _____

AUTHOR _____

TITLE _____

BETWEEN THE LINES AND BEHIND THE LINES

A HIDDEN MESSAGE ?

WHAT DO YOU THINK THE AUTHOR WAS TRYING TO SAY TO YOU?

_____
_____
_____
_____
_____
_____

DID THE AUTHOR, THROUGH THE STORY, MANAGE TO TELL YOU ANYTHING ABOUT YOURSELF THAT YOU HAD NOT THOUGHT ABOUT BEFORE?

_____
_____
_____
_____
_____
_____

WHAT SORT OF PERSON DO YOU THINK THE AUTHOR MUST BE TO WRITE A BOOK LIKE THIS?
Young / old / kind / nice / caring / friendly / understanding / lonely / miserable / unhappy / sensitive / knows what young people think and feel / out of touch / full of laughter

_____
_____
_____
_____
_____
_____

BETWEEN THE LINES AND BEHIND THE LINES

This activity encourages children to articulate their response to a story and to consider what the author's intention may have been in writing it.

STORIES

AVERY, Gillian *Mouldy's Orphan* (Puffin)
BURGESS, Melvin *The Earth Giant* (Puffin)
BYARS, Betsy *The Eighteenth Emergency* (Puffin)
CHAMBERS, Aidan *Seal Secret* (Red Fox)
FINE, Anne *The Granny Project* (Mammoth)
FINE, Anne *The Chicken Gave It To Me* (Mammoth)
FOREMAN, Michael *Grandfather's Pencil and the Room of Stories* (Red Fox)
GARNER, Alan *The Stone Book Quartet* (Collins)
HEIDE, Florence Parry *The Shrinking of Treehorn* (Puffin)
JENNINGS, Paul *The Cabbage Patch Fib* (Puffin)
JENNINGS, Paul *Uncovered* (Puffin)
JENNINGS, Paul *The Gizmo Again* (Puffin) [short stories]
KAYE, Geraldine *Comfort Herself* (Scholastic)
KEMP, Gene *The Turbulent Term of Tyke Tiler* (Puffin)
MORPURGO, Michael *The Dancing Bear* (Collins)
PEARCE, Philippa *The Battle of Bubble and Squeak* (Puffin)
RODGERS, Mary *Freaky Friday* (Puffin)
SWINDELLS, Robert *Jacqueline Hyde* (Yearling)
VELTHUIJS, Max *Frog and the Stranger* (Andersen)
WILSON, Bob *Bing, Bang, Boogie, It's a Boy Scout* (Collins)

PICTURE BOOKS

BROWNE, Anthony *A Walk in the Park* (Walker)
BROWNE, Anthony *Willy the Wimp* and series (Walker/Red Fox)
BROWNE, Anthony *Piggybook* (Walker)
BROWNE, Anthony *Look What I've Got* (Walker)
COLE, Babette *Princess Smartypants* and other titles (Puffin)
FOREMAN, Michael *Dinosaurs and All That Rubbish* (Puffin)
FOREMAN, Michael *One World* (Red Fox)
GERAGHTY, Paul *The Hunter* (Red Fox)
HOBAN, Russell and PIENKOWSKI, Jan *M.O.L.E.* (Red Fox)
HOFFMAN, Mary *Grace and Family* (Frances Lincoln)
JAMES, Simon *Dear Greenpeace* (Walker)
McKEE, David *Not Now Bernard* (Sparrow)
McKEE, David *Snow Woman* (Beaver)
McKEE, David *Elmer the Patchwork Elephant* (Red Fox)
ONYEFULU, Obi and SAFAREWICZ, Evie *Chinye* (Frances Lincoln)
WAGNER, Jenny and BROOKS, Ron *John Brown, Rose and the Midnight Cat* (Puffin)

TAKING THE TEMPERATURE OF A BOOK

0° Blissfully Hot

0° NO GO BORED

NAME _____

AUTHOR _____

TITLE _____

EMOTIONAL THERMOMETER

OVER THE TOP !

When you read this book how did you, as the reader, feel?
Rate the book on the 0–10 thermometer scale (below) and try to explain why (opposite).

10
9
8
7
6
5
4
3
2
1

HOT

My emotions ran really high. I couldn't put it down, I didn't want it to end because

_____
_____
_____
_____
_____
_____

LUKEWARM

I thought it was good but I couldn't get all steamed up about it because

_____
_____
_____
_____
_____
_____

COLD

I felt that I wanted to finish it but it was a bit of an effort because

_____
_____
_____
_____
_____

NO GO

I only got to page _____ and didn't go on because

_____
_____
_____
_____
_____
_____

TAKING THE TEMPERATURE OF A BOOK

This is a useful activity for making visible a reader's engagement with the text. It provides evidence for talking about the 'reader' and the 'writer', and positive/negative matches. It also requires children to be specific about their reading by focusing on the features that made the book a more or less compelling experience.

You could compare and discuss the reactions of different readers to the same text.

STORIES
ANHOLT, Laurence *Cinderboy* (Orchard)
ANHOLT, Laurence *Daft Jack and the Bean Stack* (Orchard)
BANKS, Lynne Reid *The Indian in the Cupboard* and sequels (Collins)
BAWDEN, Nina *The Peppermint Pig* (Puffin)
BYARS, Betsy *The Eighteenth Emergency* (Puffin)
BLACKMAN, Marjorie *Thief!* (Corgi)
BLUME, Judy *Superfudge* (Macmillan)
CORBETT, W.J. *The Battle of Chinnbrook Wood* (Hodder)
EDWARDS, Dorothy *My Naughty Little Sister* stories (Mammoth)
FINE, Anne *How to Write Really Badly* (Mammoth)
JOHNSON, Pete *The Ghost Dog* (Yearling)
MARK, Jan *My Frog and I* (Mammoth)
MARK, Jan *Thunder and Lightnings* (Puffin)
MARK, Jan *The Coconut Quins* (Puffin)
NIMMO, Jenny *Seth and the Strangers* (Mammoth)
NIMMO, Jenny *Griffin's Castle* (Mammoth)
RODDA, Emily *Power and Glory* (Allen and Unwin)
SWINDELLS, Robert *The Go-Ahead Gang* (Puffin)
WALSH, Jill Paton *Thomas and the Tinners* (Macdonald)
WESTALL, Robert *Blitz* (Collins Lions) [four stories]
WILSON, Bob *Bing, Bang, Boogie, It's a Boy Scout* (Collins)

PICTURE BOOKS
BROWN, Ruth *Our Cat, Flossie* and other titles (Beaver)
BURNINGHAM, John *Courtney* (Red Fox)
FOX, Mem *Wilfrid Gordon McDonald Partridge* (Puffin)
HEDDERWICK, Mairi *Katie Morag* series (Red Fox)
HUGHES, Shirley *Dogger* (Red Fox)

Tick the words (below) that best describe your book character. Then make a portrait. Choose a face shape, hair and features. Cut them out, then glue them in the first empty box at the bottom of this page. Write the character's name, then try another.

identikits

FACE SHAPES	EYES	NOSE	MOUTH	EARS/EYEBROWS etc	HAIR

YOUR NAME:_____

AUTHOR:_____

TITLE: _____

SHAPE OF FACE	ROUND	SQUARE	OVAL	HEAVY JAW	BIG EARS	SMALL EARS			
HAIR	STRAIGHT	CURLY	DARK	FAIR	SHORT	LONG			
EYES	BIG	SMALL	CLOSE TOGETHER	FAR APART	HEAVY LIDS	FRIENDLY	HOSTILE	SCARED	
NOSE	BIG	SMALL	FLAT	POINTED	TILTED	AQUILINE	BROAD		
MOUTH	BIG	SMALL	SMILING	ANGRY	SAD	BEMUSED	CYNICAL		
EXPRESSION	KIND	FRIENDLY	SLY	CHEEKY	HAPPY	SAD	FUNNY		

EXAMPLES

CHARACTER'S NAME CHARACTER'S NAME CHARACTER'S NAME

IDENTIKITS

This activity offers an opportunity for readers to visualise characters and describe personalities. More features can be added to extend the range of possibilities.

Discussion and collaboration in groups or pairs will enrich and extend the activity as it requires readers to go back to the text to support their ideas and conclusions. If you enlarge the face parts on the photocopier, transfer them to acetate, then cut them out, they can be used by the children to build up portraits on an overhead projector. They can work in pairs or groups for presentation to the rest of the class.

See also: **A Letter to a Book Character, Castaway Characters, Goodies and Baddies, Zodiaction, Database Dating, Prunella Problem, This is Your Life.**

AIKEN, Joan *The Wolves of Willoughby Chase* (Puffin) **Dido Twite, Miss Slighcarp**
BAWDEN, Nina *Carrie's War* (Puffin) **Carrie**
BYARS, Betsy *The Cartoonist* (Red Fox) **Alfie**
BYARS, Betsy *Cracker Jackson* (Red Fox) **Cracker and Goat**
BYARS, Betsy *The Eighteenth Emergency* (Red Fox) **Mouse**
CLEARY, Beverley *Ramona* series (Puffin) **Ramona**
CROSS, Gillian *The Great Elephant Chase* (Puffin) **Tab, Cissie**
DANZIGER, Paula *Can You Sue Your Parents for Malpractice?* (Mammoth) **Lauren**
FINE, Anne *How to Write Really Badly* (Mammoth) **Chester, Joe**
FITZHUGH, Louise *Harriet the Spy* (Puffin) **Harriet**
GARFIELD, Leon *Smith* (Puffin) **Smith**
GARFIELD, Leon *The Stolen Watch* (Puffin) **Nick, Julie**
GEORGE, Jean *My Side of the Mountain* (Red Fox) **Sam**
HOLM, Anne *I am David* (Mammoth) **David**
LOVEDAY, John *Goodbye Buffalo Sky* (Bloomsbury) **Cappy, Alice**
LOWRY, Lois *Anastasia Krupnik* (Collins) **Anastasia**
MAHY, Margaret *The Great Piratical Rumbustification* (Puffin) **the chief robber**
MURPHY, Jill *The Worst Witch* (Puffin) **Mildred**
PILLING, Ann *Mother's Daily Scream* (Puffin) **Jake or Holly**
SWINDELLS, Robert *Jacqueline Hyde* (Yearling) **Jacqueline**

CASTAWAY CHARACTER

YOU ARE ADRIFT AT SEA ON A SMALL RAFT...
FROM ALL THE BOOKS YOU HAVE READ AND LISTED IN
YOUR READING LOG, CHOOSE ONE CHARACTER TO BE
YOUR COMPANION. WHAT SORT OF PERSON WOULD YOU
CHOOSE? THE SUN IS HOT AND YOUR SUPPLIES ARE
MEAGRE....

Who? Character _____
From (title): _____
By: _____

Why? _____

_____
_____
_____
_____
_____

CASTAWAY CHARACTERS

Here, readers work out the character they would most like to have as a shipwreck companion. Answers make a good basis for group discussion in which members have to justify their choices in terms of personality, skills and temperament, based on the character's behaviour in the book they have read.

Castaway Characters can be adapted by inviting readers to choose the character they would *least* like to be stranded with. To extend the activity, children could create a composite companion, drawing on characteristics from two or three characters in different stories. This is a good way for readers to share extended independent reading of longer novels.

See also: **A Letter to a Book Character, Identikits, Goodies and Baddies, Zodiaction, Database Dating, Prunella Problem, This is Your Life.**

AIKEN, Joan *Go Saddle the Sea* (Puffin) **Felix**
AIKEN, Joan *Bridle the Wind* (Puffin) **Felix**
AIKEN, Joan *The Teeth of the Gale* (Puffin) **Felix**
BRANFORD, Henrietta *Fire, Bed, Bone* (Walker) **the dog narrator**
CARTWRIGHT, Ann and Reg *Norah's Ark* (Red Fox) **Norah**
CLEARY, Beverley *Ramona the Pest* (Puffin) **Ramona**
COOPER, Susan *The Dark is Rising* and sequels (Puffin) **Will**
DAVIES, Andrew *Conrad's War* (Scholastic) **Conrad or Dad**
CRESSWELL, Helen The *Bagthorpe* saga [any title] (Hodder) **any Bagthorpe**
CRESSWELL, Helen *The Sea Piper* (Hodder) **Harriet**
CROSS, Gilian *The Mintyglo Kid* and series (Mammoth) **Barney, Spag or Clipper**
FARMER, Penelope *Charlotte Sometimes* (Puffin) **either girl**
FINE, Anne *The Chicken Gave It To Me* (Mammoth) **Andrew or Gemma**
FIRMIN, Peter *Nina's Machines* (Collins) **Nina**
GEORGE, Jean *My Side of the Mountain* (Puffin) **Sam Bribley**
GEORGE, Jean *Julie of the Wolves* (Red Fox) **Julie**
GEORGE, Jean *Julie* (Red Fox) **Julie**
HOBAN, Russell *Tom and Captain Najork* titles (Red Fox) **Tom or Captain Najork**
JONES. Terry *Nicobobinus* (Puffin) **Nicobobinus**
KING, Clive *Stig of the Dump* (Puffin) **Stig**
MURPHY, Jill *The Worst Witch* (Puffin) **Mildred**
NAIDOO, Beverley *No Turning Back* (Puffin) **Sipho**
NORRISS, Andrew *Aquila* (Puffin) **Tom or Geoff**
SENDAK, Maurice *Where the Wild Things Are* (Collins) **Max**
SWINDELLS, Robert *World Eater* (Yearling) **Orville**
THOMAS, Ruth *Hideaway* (Red Fox) **Leah, Charlie or Jack**
WALSH, Jill Paton *Thomas and the Tinners* (Macdonald) **Thomas**
WILSON, Jacqueline *Cliffhanger* (Yearling) **Tim**

No one is 100% good or 100% bad. Choose a HERO and a VILLAIN from a book. Does the hero have faults? Does the villain have any good points? Think about what they did in the story, then colour in the graph to rank how much they showed of each quality, from 1%–100%. Add others to the list.

YOUR NAME: _____ AUTHOR: _____ TITLE: _____

GOOD CHARACTER: _____ INITIAL: _____ BAD CHARACTER: _____ INITIAL: _____

GOODIES & BADDIES GRAPH

CHARACTERISTIC	INITIAL	PERCENTAGE 0 10 20 30 40 50 60 70 80 90 100	EXAMPLE (Page)
KIND			
KIND			
GENEROUS			
GENEROUS			
CARING			
CARING			
FRIENDLY			
FRIENDLY			
HONEST			
HONEST			
THOUGHTFUL			
THOUGHTFUL			
UNSELFISH			
UNSELFISH			
TRUSTWORTHY			
TRUSTWORTHY			
MEAN			
MEAN			
JEALOUS			
JEALOUS			
SCHEMING			
SCHEMING			
ARROGANT			
ARROGANT			
DISHONEST			
DISHONEST			
THOUGHTLESS			
THOUGHTLESS			
SELFISH			
SELFISH			
UNTRUSTWORTHY			
UNTRUSTWORTHY			

INITIAL / PERCENTAGE   10   20   30   40   50   60   70   80   90   100

GOODIES AND BADDIES

Goodies and Baddies encourages empathy with behaviour and events, understanding of motivation, and evaluation of behaviour and outcomes.

Discussion may reveal ambiguities, such as villains with attractive or redeeming qualities; heroes with flaws. This activity is particularly useful in helping children discover and articulate this complexity in stories inhabited by many-layered characters (i.e. no clear-cut heroes or villains).

The patterns that emerge could provide a basis for discussion of types and stereotypes, stock characters and believable characters. The need for examples will send readers back to the text to check their readings. The activity also provides useful preparation for 'hot-seating' and other drama-based innovations.

See also: **A Letter to a Book Character, Identikits, Castaway Characters, Zodiaction, Database Dating, Prunella Problem, This is Your Life.**

ASHLEY, Bernard *Dinner Ladies Don't Count* (Puffin) **Jason, Donna, Mrs Cheff**
ALLEN, Judy *The Most Brilliant Trick Ever* (Walker) **Steve and Nick**
BYARS, Betsy *The Two Thousand Pound Goldfish* (Collins) **Warren and his mother**
BYARS, Betsy *The Eighteenth Emergency* (Red Fox) **Mouse and Hammerman**
CHAMBERS, Aidan *Seal Secret* (Red Fox) **William and Glynn**
CHAMBERS, Aidan *The Present Takers* (Red Fox) **Lucy and Melanie**
LOVEDAY, John *Goodbye Buffalo Sky* (Bloomsbury) **Long Shadow and Alice or Cappy**
LEESON, Robert *Tom's Private War* (Puffin) **Tom and William**
MARK, Jan *The Coconut Quins* (Puffin) **Zena and Paul**
MORPURGO, Michael *The Marble Crusher* (Mammoth) **Albert and Sid**
ROWLING, J.K. *Harry Potter and the Philosopher's Stone* (Bloomsbury) **Harry and Voldemort**
THOMAS, Ruth *Hideaway* (Red Fox) **Leah, Charlie, Jack, George**

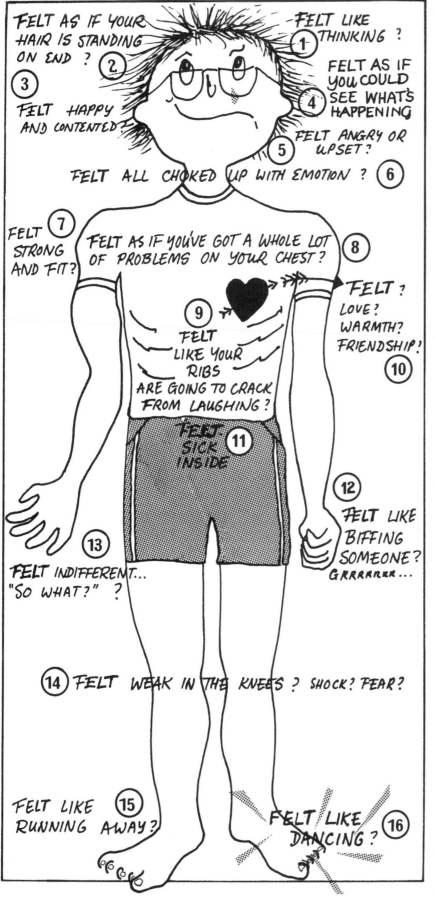

FELT AS IF YOUR HAIR IS STANDING ON END ? ②

③

FELT HAPPY AND CONTENTED?

① FELT LIKE THINKING ?

④ FELT AS IF YOU COULD SEE WHAT'S HAPPENING

⑤ FELT ANGRY OR UPSET?

FELT ALL CHOKED UP WITH EMOTION ? ⑥

⑦ FELT STRONG AND FIT?

FELT AS IF YOU'VE GOT A WHOLE LOT OF PROBLEMS ON YOUR CHEST? ⑧

⑨ FELT LIKE YOUR RIBS ARE GOING TO CRACK FROM LAUGHING ?

⑩ FELT ? LOVE? WARMTH? FRIENDSHIP!

⑪ FELT SICK INSIDE

⑫ FELT LIKE BIFFING SOMEONE? GRRRRRR...

⑬ FELT INDIFFERENT... "SO WHAT?" ?

⑭ FELT WEAK IN THE KNEES ? SHOCK? FEAR?

⑮ FELT LIKE RUNNING AWAY?

FELT LIKE DANCING ? ⑯

reading is feeling

NAME : _____

When I read _____

_____

by _____

I felt ◯ when _____

_____

_____

I felt ◯ when _____

_____

I felt ◯ when _____

_____

I felt ◯ when _____

_____

I felt ◯ when _____

_____

I felt ◯ when _____

_____

_____

IF YOU FELT ANY OF THE EMOTIONS SHOWN ON THE MAP, FILL IN THE NUMBER IN THE ◯ ABOVE AND SAY WHEN.

READING IS FEELING

Identifying significant moments in a narrative helps readers to articulate their responses. The sixteen different emotions given on this sheet provide a basic vocabulary for children who are unaccustomed to identifying and expressing such feelings.

Talking in small groups or pairs, comparing and sharing their responses will help the children to extend and refine what they feel. *Reading is Feeling* can also provide a first step towards keeping a response log or journal.

See also: **Reading as Feeling.**

STORIES

ALLEN, Judy *The Most Brilliant Trick Ever* (Walker)

ASHTON, Jay *Keeping Cats* (Oxford)

DEARY, Terry *True Ghost Stories* (Scholastic)

DOHERTY, Berlie *Willa and Old Mrs Anna* (Walker)

GAVIN, Jamila *Someone's Watching, Someone's Waiting* (Mammoth)

GARNER, Alan *Tom Fobble's Day* [last of the Stone Book quartet] (Collins)

GERAS, Adele *My Grandmother's Stories* (Mammoth)

HALLWORTH, Grace (ed.) *Mermaid and Monster: Stories From the Sea* (Mammoth)

HOBAN, Russell *The Mouse and His Child* (Puffin)

HUGHES, Ted *The Iron Man* (Faber)

KING-SMITH, Dick *Harriet's Hare* (Yearling)

MORPURGO, Michael *The Wreck of the Zanzibar* (Mammoth)

KLEIN, Robin *Dresses of Red and Gold* (Puffin) [linked short stories]

MARK, Jan *My Frog and I* (Mammoth)

MORPURGO, Michael *The Dancing Bear* (Collins)

MORPURGO, Michael *Why the Whales Came* (Mammoth)

NIMMO, Jenny *The Owl Tree* (Walker)

SUTCLIFF, Rosemary *Beowulf: Dragon Slayer* (Red Fox)

SWINDELLS, Robert *Hurricane Summer* (Mammoth)

WALSH, Jill Paton *Thomas and the Tinners* (Macdonald)

WESTALL, Robert *The Christmas Cat* (Mammoth)

WHITE, E.B. *Charlotte's Web* (Puffin)

WILLIAMS, Ursula Moray *The Adventures of the Little Wooden Horse* (Puffin)

PICTURE BOOKS

BLAKE, Quentin *Clown* (Red Fox)

BAKER, Jeannie *Where the Forest Meets the Sea* (Walker)

HEIDE, Florence Parry and GILLILAND, Judith Heide; ill. by Ted Lewin *The Day of Ahmed's Secret* (Gollancz)

MURPHY, Jill *A Piece of Cake* (Walker)

MURPHY, Jill *Five Minutes Peace* (Walker)

STEPTOE, John *Mufaro's Beautiful Daughters* (Puffin)

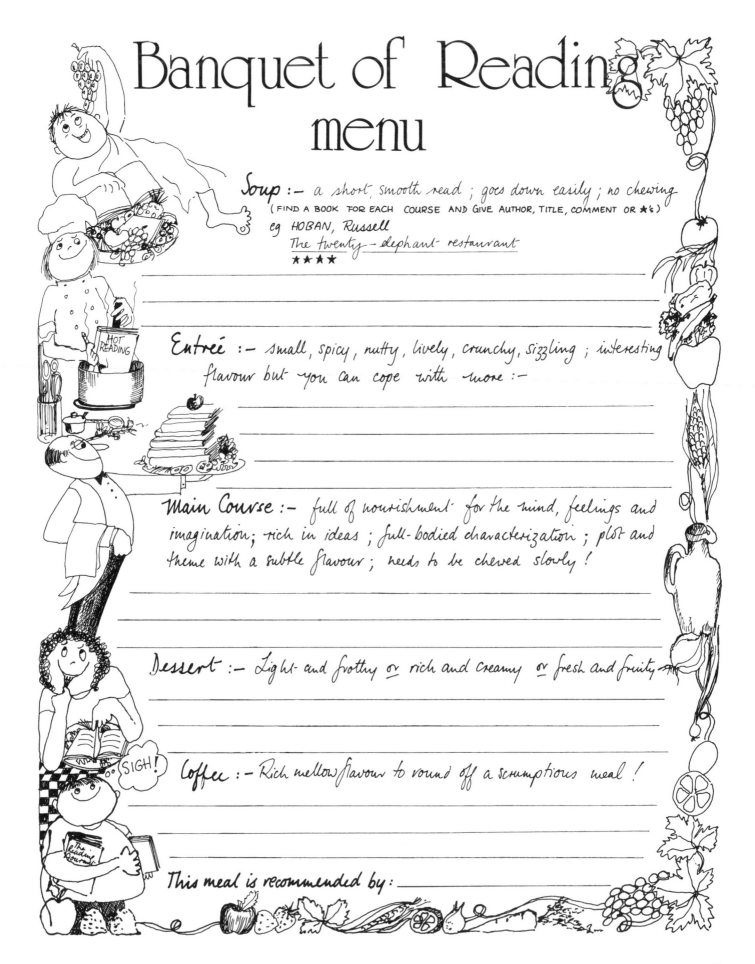

Banquet of Reading menu

Soup :- a short, smooth read ; goes down easily ; no chewing
(FIND A BOOK FOR EACH COURSE AND GIVE AUTHOR, TITLE, COMMENT OR ✶'s)
eg HOBAN, Russell
The twenty - elephant - restaurant
★ ★ ★ ★

_____
_____
_____

Entrée :- small, spicy, nutty, lively, crunchy, sizzling ; interesting flavour but you can cope with more :-

_____
_____
_____

Main Course :- full of nourishment for the mind, feelings and imagination; rich in ideas ; full-bodied characterization ; plot and theme with a subtle flavour ; needs to be chewed slowly !

_____
_____
_____

Dessert :- Light and frothy or rich and creamy or fresh and fruity

_____
_____
_____

Coffee :- Rich mellow flavour to round off a scrumptious meal !

_____
_____
_____

This meal is recommended by : _____

BANQUET OF READING

Making up a menu encourages children to review their reading, characterise the different kinds of pleasure that stories offer and to share their particular favourites. The book list below contains my personal favourites which I'd like to share with all children; but everyone will have their own preferences.

See also: **Alphabetical Authors, Booktails, Country Couples.**

SOUP: a short, smooth read - picture books with appeal for all ages.
AHLBERG, Allan; ill. by Janet Ahlberg *Mrs Wobble the Waitress* (Puffin)
AHLBERG, Allan; ill. by Colin McNaughton *Miss Brick the Builder's Baby* (Puffin)
AHLBERG, Allan; ill. by Emma Chichester Clark *Mrs Vole the Vet* (Puffin)
AHLBERG, Allan; ill. by Tony Ross *Miss Dirt the Dustman's Daughter* (Puffin)
BLAKE, Quentin *The Story of the Dancing Frog* (Red Fox)
BLAKE, Quentin *Mr Magnolia* (Red Fox)
BLAKE, Quentin *Two Cockatoos* (Red Fox)
BURNINGHAM, John *Would You Rather; Courtney* and all the others (Red Fox)
HEIDE, Florence Parry *The Shrinking of Treehorn* (Puffin)
HOBAN, Russell and BLAKE, Quentin *How Tom Beat Captain Najork and His Hired Sportsmen* (Red Fox)
SENDAK, Maurice *Where the Wild Things Are* (Collins)

ENTREE: small, spicy, nutty, crunchy, sizzling - whets reading appetite.
AHLBERG, Alan and Janet *Jeremiah in the Dark Woods* (Puffin)
AHLBERG, Alan and Janet *It Was a Dark and Stormy Night* (Puffin)
CAMERON, Ann *Julian Stories* (Yearling)
FINE, Anne *Bill's New Frock* (Mammoth)
LAVELLE, Sheila *My Best Fiend* and series (Puffin)
LOBEL, Arnold *Frog and Toad* stories (Mammoth)
PEARCE, Philippa *What the Neighbours Did* (Puffin) [short stories]
HUGHES, Ted *The Iron Man* (Faber)

MAIN COURSE: meaty nourishment for the mind, feelings and imagination - to chew over and relish.
BAWDEN, Nina *The Peppermint Pig* (Puffin)
COOPER, Susan *The Dark is Rising* and sequels (Puffin)
GARDAM, Jane *The Hollow Land* (Walker)
GARNER, Alan *The Stone Book* quartet (Collins)
HOBAN, Russell *The Mouse and His Child* (Puffin)
HOLM, Ann *I am David* (Puffin)
HOWKER, JANNI *Badger on the Barge* [short stories] (Walker)
KEMP, Gene *The Turbulent Term of Tyke Tiler* (Puffin)
PEARCE, Philippa *The Way to Sattin Shore* (Puffin)
PEARCE, Philippa *Tom's Midnight Garden* (Puffin)

DESSERT AND COFFEE - a little something to delight and amuse.
BROWNE, Anthony *Piggybook* (Walker)
HOBAN, Russell *Dinner at Alberta's* (Puffin)
LEESON, Robert *Never Kiss Frogs* (Puffin)
MARSHALL, James *Three by the Sea* (Red Fox)
MURPHY, Jill *Five Minutes Peace* (Walker); *A Piece of Cake* (Walker)
ROSS, Tony Any title
SCIESZKA, John *The True Story of the Wolf and the Three Little Pigs* (Puffin)
SCIESZKA, John *The Stinky Cheese Man and Other Stories* (Puffin)

bookburgers reading recipe

The best bookburgers are made with only the best ingredients.
Choose a book and test the ingredients . . .

chef: _____ author: _____

title: _____

ingredients: Rich, beefy, full-flavoured characters ... so clear you feel as if you
know them. Give examples :—

_____

_____

Mixed with : speech, dialogue so clear you feel you can hear them. Quote example :—

_____

_____

Spiced with : description of places so clear you can see them. Quote example :—

_____

_____

Blended into : a subtle plot with an interesting flavour and some surprises. What is it?

_____

_____

Topped with a unique sauce. What makes it different, better for you than others ?

_____

Delicious
Nutritious
Finger-licking
food for the
imagination

Served on a bed of crunchy fresh language with a relish of words like:—

_____

_____

Exchange recipes with a friend. Become a connoisseur of bookburgers.

BOOKBURGERS READING RECIPE

This lively alternative to the standard book review offers a framework that helps readers focus on specific aspects, such as character, setting, dialogue, plot structure, language/vocabulary and personal response. Requests for quotations and examples send the reader back to the text.

The finished recipes provide a basis for group discussion and comparison. They also serve as recommendations to other book consumers in the class.

AHLBERG, Allan *Woof!* (Puffin)
AIKEN, Joan *The Winter Sleepwalker* (Red Fox)
ALCOCK, Vivien *Travellers by Night* (Mammoth)
AIKEN, Joan *Cold Shoulder Road* (Red Fox)
ASHTON, Jay *Keeping Cats* (Oxford)
BROWN, Jeff *Flat Stanley's Adventures* (Mammoth)
CORBETT, W.J. *The Battle of Chinnbrook Wood* (Hodder)
CRESSWELL, Helen *Bag of Bones* (Hodder)
CROSS, Gillian *The Great Elephant Chase* (Puffin)
DOHERTY, Berlie *How Green You Are* (Mammoth)
HARKER, Lesley *Carlos and Little Wolf* (Red Fox)
HATHORN, Libby and ROGERS, Gregory *Way Home* (Red Fox)
HENDRY, Diana *The Thing-in-a-box* (Collins)
HENDRY, Diana *The Thing-on-two-legs* (Collins)
JONES, Terry *The Saga of Erik the Viking* (Puffin)
JONES, Terry *Nicobobinus* (Puffin)
KEMP, Gene *Dog's Journey* (Collins)
KING-SMITH, Dick *Harriet's Hare* (Transworld)
LAVELLE, Sheila *My Best Fiend* series (Puffin)
LIVELY, Penelope *Staying with Grandpa* (Puffin)
MARK, Jan *A Worm's Eye View* (Mammoth)
MORPURGO, Michael *The Wreck of the Zanzibar* (Mammoth)
OAKLEY, Graham *The Church Mice/Cat* series (Macmillan)
PEYTON, K.M. *The Pony That Went to Sea* (Mammoth)
SCOTT, Hugh *The Camera Obscura* (Walker)
WALSH, Jill Paton *Thomas and the Tinners* (Macdonald)
WILSON, Jacqueline *Cliffhanger* (Yearling)
WILSON, Jacqueline *Double Act* (Yearling)

zodiaction

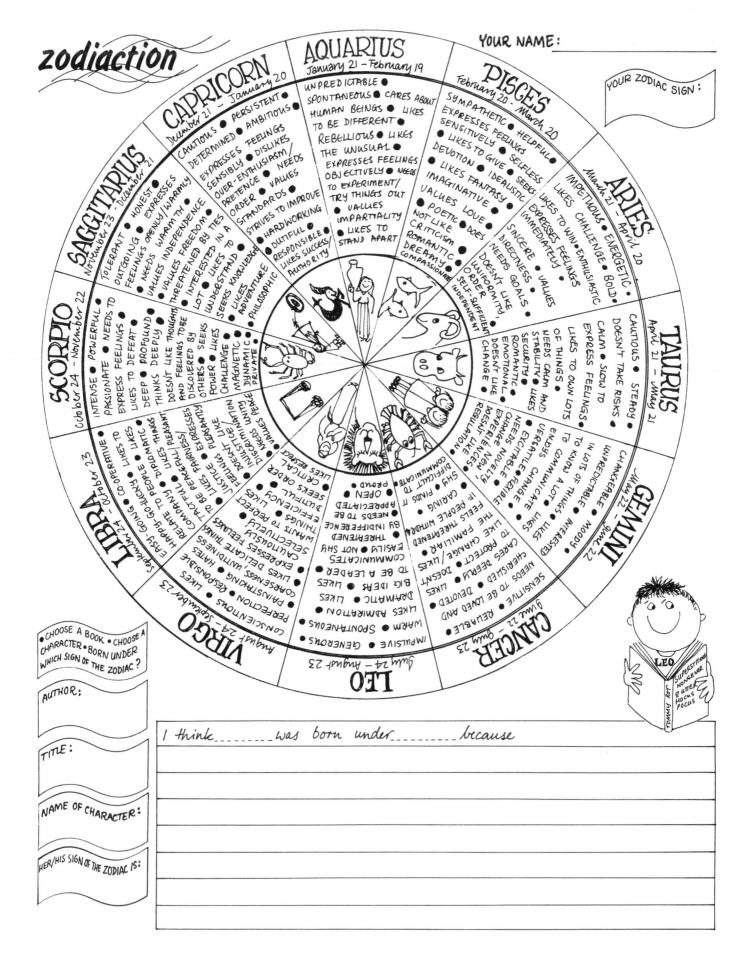

YOUR ZODIAC SIGN:

AQUARIUS January 21 – February 19
UNPREDICTABLE • SPONTANEOUS • CARES ABOUT HUMAN BEINGS • LIKES TO BE DIFFERENT • REBELLIOUS • LIKES THE UNUSUAL • EXPRESSES FEELINGS OBJECTIVELY • NEEDS TO EXPERIMENT/TRY THINGS OUT • VALUES IMPARTIALITY • LIKES TO STAND APART

CAPRICORN December 21 – January 20
CAUTIOUS • PERSISTENT • DETERMINED • AMBITIOUS • EXPRESSES FEELINGS SENSIBLY • DISLIKES OVER-ENTHUSIASM/PRETENCE • NEEDS ORDER • VALUES STANDARDS • STRIVES TO IMPROVE • HARDWORKING • DUTIFUL • RESPONSIBLE • LIKES SUCCESS/AUTHORITY

SAGGITARIUS November 23 – December 21
HONEST • EXPRESSES FEELINGS OPENLY/WARMLY • NEEDS WARMTH • VALUES INDEPENDENCE • VALUES FREEDOM • THREATENED BY TIES • INTERESTED IN A LOT • LIKES TO UNDERSTAND • SEEKS KNOWLEDGE • LIKES ADVENTURE • PHILOSOPHIC • TOLERANT • OUTGOING

PISCES February 20 – March 20
SYMPATHETIC • HELPFUL • EXPRESSES FEELINGS SENSITIVELY • SELFLESS • LIKES TO GIVE • SEEKS DEVOTION • IDEALISTIC • LIKES FANTASY • IMAGINATIVE • VALUES LOVE • POETIC • DOES NOT LIKE CRITICISM • ROMANTIC • DREAMY • COMPASSIONATE

ARIES March 21 – April 20
IMPETUOUS • ENERGETIC • BOLD • LIKES CHALLENGE • ENTHUSIASTIC • LIKES TO WIN • EXPRESSES FEELINGS IMMEDIATELY

SCORPIO October 24 – November 22
INTENSE • POWERFUL • PASSIONATE • NEEDS TO EXPRESS FEELINGS • LIKES TO DEFEAT • PROFOUND • THINKS DEEPLY • DOESN'T LIKE THOUGHTS DISCOVERED BY OTHERS • SEEKS POWER • LIKES CHALLENGE • MAGNETIC • DYNAMIC • PRIVATE

TAURUS April 21 – May 21
CAUTIOUS • STEADY • DOESN'T TAKE RISKS • CALM • SLOW TO EXPRESS FEELINGS • LIKES TO OWN LOTS OF THINGS • NEEDS CALM AND SECURITY • VALUES STABILITY • LIKES DIRECTION • NEEDS GOALS • SINCERE • DOESN'T LIKE CHANGE • UNIFORMITY/ORDER • SELF-SUFFICIENT • INDEPENDENT

LIBRA September 24 – October 23
CO-OPERATIVE • LIKES PEOPLE • EASY-GOING • LIKES TO BE DIPLOMATIC • HAPPY TO PLEASE • RELATES TO PEOPLE • LIKES COMPANY • TACTFUL • PEACEFUL • LIKES TO BE FAIR • EXPRESSES FAIRNESS • UNJUSTICE • REBELLIOUS • DISTASTE FOR INJUSTICE/DISCRIMINATION • SEEKS PEACE • VALUES PEACE • LIKES PLEASANT THINGS

GEMINI May 22 – June 22
CHANGEABLE • UNPREDICTABLE • INTERESTED • LIKES NOVELTY • VERSATILE • FLEXIBLE • EXCITABLE • LIKES CHANGE • ENERGETIC • RESTLESS • EXPERIMENTS • CHANGES NOW • DOESN'T LIKE ROUTINE • EMOTIONAL • DIFFICULT TO COMMUNICATE • IN LOTS OF THINGS • LIKES TO KNOW A LOT • NEEDS TO COMMUNICATE • SHY FINDS IT DIFFICULT TO COMMUNICATE • MOODY

VIRGO August 24 – September 23
CONSCIENTIOUS • PERFECTION • RESPONSIBLE • HATES PAINSTAKING • CARES UNTIDINESS • EXPRESSES DELICATE FEELINGS • SELECTIVELY LIKES THINGS TO BE PERFECT • WANTS TO PERFECT • CAUTIOUSLY LIKES EFFICIENCY • LIKES BIG IDEAS • LIKES TO BE A LEADER

LEO July 24 – August 23
GENEROUS • IMPULSIVE • WARM • SPONTANEOUS • LIKES ADMIRATION • DRAMATIC • LIKES TO BE A LEADER • OPEN • PROUD • NEEDS TO BE APPRECIATED • THREATENED BY INDIFFERENCE • EASILY COMMUNICATES • NOT SHY • IF PEOPLE WITHDRAW • FEELS THREATENED

CANCER June 22 – July 23
SENSITIVE • RELIABLE • NEEDS TO BE LOVED AND CHERISHED • DEVOTED • DEEPLY CARES • DOESN'T LIKES PROTECT/CHANGE • CARING • LIKE FAMILIAR

• CHOOSE A BOOK • CHOOSE A CHARACTER • CHOOSE A BORN UNDER WHICH SIGN OF THE ZODIAC?

AUTHOR:

TITLE:

NAME OF CHARACTER:

HER/HIS SIGN OF THE ZODIAC IS:

I think _____ was born under _____ because

ZODIACTION

More suitable for older readers who are familiar with astrology/horoscopes, this activity offers another way to analyse and think about characters. The characteristics provided on the chart are *not* meant to be taken seriously; they are designed to act as a catalyst for discussion of interesting book characters.

If several readers are working on the same character, it is interesting for them to compare their analyses. Can they justify their choice by reference to behaviour and events, motivation and outcomes?

See also: **A Letter to a Book Character, Identikits, Castaway Characters, Goodies and Baddies, Database Dating, Prunella Problem, This is Your Life.**

AIKEN, Joan *Go Saddle the Sea* and sequels (Red Fox) **Felix**
AIKEN, Joan *Wolves of Willoughby Chase* and sequels (Red Fox) **Dido Twite**
ASHLEY,Bernard *Dinner Ladies Don't Count* (Puffin) **Jason**
ASHLEY, Chris *Wasim in the Deep End* (Red Fox) **Wasim**
BYARS, Betsy *The Eighteenth Emergency* (Red Fox) **Mouse**
CLEARY, Beverley *Ramona* stories (Puffin) **Ramona**
DAHL, Roald *Danny the Champion of the World* (Puffin) **Danny, his father**
DAHL, Roald *Fantastic Mr Fox* (Puffin) **Mr Fox**
FINE, Anne *How to Write Really Badly* (Mammoth) **Chester or Joe**
FIRMIN, Peter *Nina's Machines* (Collins) **Nina**
GEORGE, Jean *Julie of the Wolves* (Red Fox) **Julie or Miyax**
KEMP, Gene *The Turbulent Term of Tyke Tiler* (Puffin) **Tyke**
LINGARD, Joan *The Twelfth Day of July* (Puffin) **Sadie, Nick, Kevin**
MARK, Jan *Thunder and Lightnings* (Puffin) **Andrew, Victor**
MARK, Jan *A Worm's Eye View* (Mammoth) **Alice**
MORPURGO, Michael *The Wreck of the Zanzibar* (Mammoth) **Laura**
NIMMO, Jenny *Griffin's Castle* (Mammoth) **Dinah**
PEARCE, Philippa *The Way to Sattin Shore* (Puffin) **Kate**
ROY, Jacqueline *Fat Chance* (Puffin) **Tessa, Jasper**
SUTCLIFF, Rosemary *The High Deeds of Finn McCool* (Red Fox) **Finn**
SWINDELLS, Robert *Jacqueline Hyde* (Yearling) **Jacqueline**
WILSON, Jacqueline *Cliffhanger* (Yearling) **Tim, Biscuits**

Prunella Problem
COLUMNIST,
COUNSELLOR,
FRIEND

NAME: _____

Imagine that you are a character in the book you have just read. Write a letter to Prunella's column describing your situation and asking for advice. Write Prunella's reply yourself, or give it to a friend to reply if she/he has also read the book.

TITLE: _____

PRUNELLA PROBLEM AUTHOR: _____

Dear Miss Problem of Prunella's Problem Page,
  My name is _____ and I am writing to you because I've got this big problem. _____
_____
_____
_____
_____
_____
_____
_____
_____
_____
_____
                                    Signed _____

Reply   Dear _____
_____
_____
_____
_____
_____
_____
_____
_____
_____
_____
        With my best wishes, Prunella Problem

PRUNELLA PROBLEM

Prunella Problem offers a framework to help the reader engage with a character. One pupil can write both the letter and its reply; or two pupils who have read the same book can take turns with the roles, one being the letter writer and the other being Prunella Problem. Alternatively, a group could discuss how Prunella Problem might answer a letter from another group.

See also: **A Letter to a Book Character, Identikits, Castaway Characters, Goodies and Baddies, Zodiaction, Database Dating, This is Your Life.**

ALCOCK, Vivienne *The Cuckoo Sister* (Collins)
BLUME, Judy *Are You There, God, It's Me Margaret* (Macmillan)
BLUME, Judy *Superfudge* (Macmillan)
BLUME, Judy *Then Again Maybe I Won't* (Macmillan)
BLUME, Judy *The Pain and the Great One* (Macmillan)
BYARS, Betsy *The Eighteenth Emergency* and other titles (Red Fox)
CRESSWELL, Helen *The Sea Piper* (Hodder)
DANZIGER, Paula *Can You Sue Your Parents for Malpractice?* (Mammoth)
DANZIGER, Paula *The Cat Ate My Gymsuit* (Mammoth)
DANZIGER, Paula *The Divorce Express* (Mammoth)
FINE, Anne *The Granny Project* (Mammoth)
GAVIN, Jamila *I Want to be An Angel* and other stories (Mammoth)
GLEITZMAN, Morris *Two Weeks With the Queen* (Macmillan)
LOVEDAY, John *Goodbye Buffalo Sky* (Bloomsbury)
MARK, Jan *A Worm's Eye View* (Mammoth)
MARK, Jan *The Coconut Quins* (Puffin)
MARK, Jan *Dead Letter Box* (Young Puffin)
MARK, Jan *Handles* (Puffin)
McALLISTER, Margaret *A Friend for Rachel* (Oxford)
MORPURGO, Michael *The Marble Crusher* (Mammoth)
PILLING, Ann *Mother's Daily Scream* (Puffin)
ROWLING, J.K. *Harry Potter and the Philosopher's Stone* (Bloomsbury)
ROY, Jacqueline *Fat Chance* (Puffin)
SWINDELLS, Robert *The Hurricane Summer* (Mammoth)
WILSON, Jacqueline *Cliffhanger* and other titles (Yearling)
YEOMAN, John *The Glove Puppet Man* (Collins)

DATABASE DATING

Your name: ....

AUTHOR ....

TITLE ....

BOOK CHARACTER'S NAME ....

CHARACTER ANALYSIS

PHYSICAL		PERSONALITY	
Female		Pleasant	
Male		Friendly	
Short		Kind	
Tall		Helpful	
Dark		Loving	
Fair		Fair	
Slim		Gentle	
Sturdy		Full of laughter	
Thin		Responsible	
Weedy		Sincere	
Pretty		Steady	
Handsome		Placid	
Lithe		Happy	
Slow moving		Well balanced	
Plain		Generous	
Ordinary looking		Thoughtful	
Special looking		Unpleasant	
Stunning		Unfriendly	
All round average		Unkind	
		Obnoxious	
Other		Rude	
		Unlovable	
OVERALL CHARACTER TYPE		Tough	
Extrovert, gregarious		Mean	
Introvert, loner		Unfair	
Warm, bubbly, friendly		Insincere	
Shy, withdrawn, silent		Serious, no humour	
Steady, hardworking, reliable		Impetuous	
Impulsive, flipperty, fun		Unhappy	
Emotional, shows feelings		Jealous	
Reserved, deep feelings		Silly	
Arty, imaginative		Thoughtless	
Hearty, sporty		Selfish	
Indoor type		Irresponsible	
Outdoor type		Spiteful	
		Conscientious	
		Scatterbrain	

AGE ....

NATIONALITY ....

DATABASE DATING

The idea of this activity is to have fun and stimulate talk about characters. The reader starts by ticking the words that most aptly describe their chosen character. You can then take the activity in several different ways:

To select the most similar partner for their chosen character, one child could read out the characteristics he or she has ticked on the analysis chart, while the others in the group count each time a tick coincides with a characteristic they have ticked for their character. Using a computer, a group could design fields, enter data on book characters and interrogate the database. They could also find the pair who are most dissimilar.

Extend the activity into writing or drama by asking children to imagine their chosen characters meeting for the first time and to base their behaviour on what they know of them.

See also: **A Letter to a Book Character, Identikits, Castaway Characters, Goodies and Baddies, Zodiaction, Prunella Problem, This is Your Life.**

FEMALE CHARACTERS
AHLBERG, Allan *Happy Families* series (Puffin) **Miss Dose the Doctor's Daughter; Mrs Plug the Plumber
or any other females**
CLEARY, Beverley *Ramona the Pest* (Puffin) **Ramona the Pest**
CROSS, Gillian *The Great Elephant Chase* (Puffin) **Cissie**
DAHL, Roald *Matilda* (Puffin) **Matilda**
DAHL, Roald *Revolting Rhymes* (Puffin) or a traditional form of Red Riding Hood **Red Riding Hood**
EDWARDS, Dorothy *My Naughty Little Sister* (Mammoth) **My Naughty Little Sister**
HEDDERWICK, Mairi *Katie Morag* stories (Red Fox) **Katie Morag's Grannies**
HOBAN, Russel *Tom and Captain Najork* stories (Red Fox) **Aunt Fidget Wonkham-Strong;
Miss Bundlejoy Cosysweet**
LAVELLE, Sheila *My Best Fiend* and series (Puffin) **the Fiend**
LINDGREN, Astrid *Pippi Longstocking* (Puffin) **Pippi Longstocking**
MARK, Jan *Coconut Quins* (Puffin) **Zena**
MORPURGO, Michael *The Wreck of the Zanzibar* (Mammoth) **Laura**
ROY, Jaqueline *Fat Chance* (Puffin) **Tessa**
THOMAS, Ruth *Hideaway* (Red Fox) **Leah**

MALE CHARACTERS
BRIGGS, Raymond *Father Christmas* (Puffin) **Father Christmas**
COLE, Babette *Prince Cinders* (Puffin) **Prince Cinders**
DAHL, Roald *The BFG* (Puffin) **the BFG**
GRAHAME, Kenneth *Wind in the Willows* (Puffin) **Toad**
HEIDE, Florence Parry *The Shrinking of Treehorn* (Puffin) **Treehorn**
HOBAN, Russell *Dinner at Alberta's* (Puffin) **Arthur**
HUGHES, Ted *The Iron Man* (Faber) **the Iron Man**
LIVELY, Penelope *The Ghost of Thomas Kempe* (Puffin) **the Ghost**
McCAUGHREAN, Geraldine *Cowboy Jess* (Dolphin) **Cowboy Jess**
POTTER, Beatrix *The Tale of Peter Rabbit* (Warne/Puffin) **Peter Rabbit**
ROWLING, J.K. *Harry Potter and the Philosopher's Stone* (Bloomsbury) **Harry Potter**
THOMAS, Rugh *Hideaway* (Red Fox) **Jack**
WALSH, Jill Paton *Thomas and the Tinners* (Macdonald) **Thomas**
WILSON, Bob *Stanley Bagsaw and the Twenty-two Ton Whale* (Puffin) **Stanley Bagshaw**

THIS IS YOUR LIFE!

Dear ....,

We are putting together a THIS IS YOUR LIFE programme on ....

Please could you assist us by completing the following biographical details:

Born (approximate or exact date) .... Siblings ....

Where (town, country) ....

Parents .... Brought up by ....

Education ....

Achievements ....

....

....

....

....

....

....

....

....

....

....

....

We would appreciate it if you would list the people whom you think should be invited to appear on the programme and say how and why he or she was important in the life of this person:

NAME ....

Why ....

....

NAME ....

Why ....

....

NAME ....

Why ....

....

THIS IS YOUR LIFE

You can undertake this activity using biographies, autobiographies, fictionalised fact, and fiction written in the style of biography or autobiography. The non-fiction route can lead to comparison of information from more than one source.

The results lend themselves to various extensions and adaptations such as: role play, in which the researcher has to persuade the producer that a particular character should appear on the programme; interviewing the character on a chat show; making a programme for radio or television, with other pupils acting out significant characters in the person's life; or writing a newspaper profile or obituary.

See also: **A Letter to a Book Character, Identikits, Castaway Characters, Goodies and Baddies, Zodiaction, Database Dating, Prunella Problem.**

FICTION

ALCOTT, Louisa *Little Women* (several publishers)
CUSHMAN, Karen *The Midwife's Apprentice* (Macmillan)
DOHERTY, Berlie *Granny was a Buffer Girl* (Mammoth)
GEORGE, Jean *Julie of the Wolves* (Red Fox)
GEORGE, Jean *Julie* (Red Fox)
LEESON, Robert *The Story of Robin of Sherwood* (Kingfisher)
MacLACHLAN, Patricia *Sarah, Plain and Tall* (Puffin)
MacLACHLAN, Patricia *Skylark* (Collins)
MORPURGO, Michael *Arthur, High King of Britain* (Mammoth)
MORPURGO, Michael *The Wreck of the Zanzibar* (Mammoth)
PEARCE, Philippa and FAIRFAX-LUCY, Brian *The Children of Charlecote* (Gollancz)
SIMPSON, Margaret *Top Ten Arthurian Legends* (Scholastic)
STREATFEILD, Noel *Ballet Shoes* (Puffin)
SUTCLIFF, Rosemary *Beowulf: Dragon Slayer* (Red Fox)
SUTCLIFF, Rosemary *The High Deeds of Finn McCool* (Red Fox)
URE, Jean *Becky Bananas This is Your Life* (Collins)
WADDELL, Martin and DUPASQUIER, Philippe *Going West* (Puffin)
YEOMAN, John (ed) and BLAKE, Quentin *Sinbad the Sailor* (Pavilion)

NON-FICTION

BAKER, Nicola *Jane Austen* (Evans)
DAHL, Roald *Boy* [autobiography] (Puffin)
DAHL, Roald *Going Solo* [autobiography] (Puffin)
FOREMAN, Michael *War Boy* (Puffin)
FOREMAN, Michael *When the War Was Over* (Puffin)
Various authors *Heroes from the East* series (Hood Hood Books)
KERR, Judith *Out of the Hitler Time* (Collins)
KERR, Judith *When Hitler Stole Pink Rabbit* (Collins)
KERR, Judith *A Small Person Far Away* (Collins)
MALARY, John *Vincent Van Gogh* (Evans)
POLLARD, Michael *Emmeline Pankhurst* (Evans)
POWLING, Chris *Roald Dahl* (Evans)
ROSS, Stewart *William Shakespeare* (Evans)
Various authors *What's their story?* series (Oxford) [features Dahl, Ghandi,
         Shakespeare, Captain Cook]

COUNTRY COUPLES

Read the books suitable for your age group and try to pair the two set in the same country:

TITLE	TITLE	COUNTRY
Example: GEE, Maurice, *Under the mountain* (Puffin)	De Hamel, Joan *X marks the spot* (Puffin)	New Zealand
Book 1	Book 2	
Book 1	Book 2	
Book 1	Book 2	
Book 1	Book 2	
Book 1	Book 2	
Book 1	Book 2	

COUNTRY COUPLES

This activity focuses on the geographical setting of different stories and can be used to extend the range and variety of reading material, including atlases, the Internet, newspapers and so on. There are opportunities for discussing and evaluating how writers present setting, and different kinds of writing.

Using the format of *Country Couples*, other kinds of pairs can be found to suit the reading preferences and needs of your class, such as books with matching historical settings. There are also good opportunities to to explore the fact/fiction relationship.

Listed below are a few books to get you started with non-British locations, but also look at settings in different parts of the UK.

See also: **Alphabetical Authors, Booktails, Banquet of Reading.**

STORIES
CROSS, Gillian *The Great Elephant Chase* (Puffin) **USA**
GEORGE, Jean *Julie of the Wolves* (Red Fox) **Inuit**
GEORGE, Jean *Julie* (Red Fox) **Inuit**
GERAGHTY, Paul *The Hunter* (Red Fox) **Africa**
JAFFREY, Madhur *Seasons of Splendour* (Puffin) **India**
KAYE, Geraldine *Comfort Herself* (Scholastic) **Ghana**
LINDEN, Anne Marie; ill. by DOYLE, Katherine *Emerald Blue* (Mammoth) **Caribbean**
LOVEDAY, John *Goodbye Buffalo Sky* (Bloomsbury) **American West**
McCAUGHREAN, Geraldine *Gold Dust* (Puffin) **Brazil**
McCAUGHREAN, Geraldine *Plundering Paradise* (Puffin) **Mozambique**
NAIDOO, Beverley *No Turning Back* (Puffin) **Johannesberg**
WILDER, Laura Ingalls *Little House* series (Puffin) **American Pioneer**

PICTURE BOOKS
BAKER, Jeannie *Where the Forest Meets the Sea* (Walker) **Queensland, Australia**
STEPTOE, John *Mufaro's Beautiful Daughters* (Puffin) **Zimbabwe**
WADDELL, Martin and DUPASQUIER, Philippe *Going West* (Puffin) **American Pioneer**

POETRY
STEWART, Pauline *Singing Down the Breadfruit* (Red Fox) **Caribbean**

STUDENT VIEW OF READING : QUESTIONNAIRE

NAME _____ CLASS _____

CROSS OUT WHAT DOES NOT APPLY

I think reading is important / I do not think reading is important
because _____
_____
_____
_____

I enjoy reading / I do not enjoy reading because _____
_____

I read a lot / I read very little because _____
_____

I prefer reading fiction / I prefer reading non-fiction / I like reading both   because
_____

Why read? What purpose does reading serve?
   To _____
   To _____
   To _____
   To _____

Do you like stories which :

		How do you feel about yourself as a reader? [Tick box]
Make you laugh?	Yes / No	
Make you cry?	Yes / No	GREAT WHOOPEE REALLY OK ☐
Make you think hard?	Yes / No	
Make you feel like the book character?	Yes / No	
Are about people like you and their problems?	Yes / No	
Are about everyday life?	Yes / No	So So SORT OF OK MIDDLING ☐
Are about friends?	Yes / No	
Are set in other countries?	Yes / No	
Are set in the past?	Yes / No	BLEH! YUK! DEPRESSED DOWN ☐
Are about animals, not people?	Yes / No	
Are about real people?	Yes / No	
Are about space, aliens, the future?	Yes / No	

FURTHER READING

BARRS, Myra and ROSEN, Michael (eds) *A Year with Poetry* (CLPE) Primary teachers talk in different ways about poetry in their classrooms.

BENTON, Michael and FOX, Geoff *Teaching Literature 9 -14* (OUP 1985) Still a very relevant guide. Practical examples and ideas rooted in sound principles. Good on response.

COOLING, Wendy *Books to Enjoy 8-12* (1998 SLA) An annotated list of over 150 titles.

ELLIS, Sue and BARRS, Myra *The Core Book: a structured approach to using books within the Reading Curriculum* (CLPE 1997) A helpful discussion of the relationship between literature and learning to read.

GRAHAM, Judith *Cracking Good Books: Teaching Literature at KS2* (NATE) Very useful.

LAZIM, Ann and MOSS, Elaine *The Core Booklist* (CLPE 1997) A companion list of titles tried and tested in the classroom.

MEEK, Margaret *How Texts Teach What Readers Learn* (Thimble Press 1988) A short, accessible exposition of the essential connections between texts we make available and learning to read.

POWLING, Chris and STYLES, Morag (eds) *A Guide to Poetry 0-13* (Books for Keeps and the Reading and Language Information Centre, Reading, 1996) Extensive bibliography plus interesting and useful articles on various aspects of poetry in school.

REVIEW SOURCES

Books for Keeps, 6 Brightfield Road, Lee, London SE12 8QF (0181 852 4953). Six issues per year. Short reviews by people in touch with children. Excellent Authorgraphs and feature articles. The liveliest and most useful journal for teachers. BfK also publishes useful guides and booklists.

Carousel, 7 Carrs Lane, Birmingham B4 7TG (0121 643 6411). Published three times a year. With its origins in the Federation of Children's Book Groups, parents are the prime audience; but reviews and wide-ranging features make this a useful and interesting publication for teachers.

OTHER SOURCES

Thimble Press, Lockwood, Station Road, Sth Woodchester, Stroud, Gloucester GL5 5EZ. Publishes **Signal**, the journal about children's literature, and occasional publications which are most relevant for thoughtful teachers of reading.

The Poetry Society, 22 Betterton Street, London WC2H 9BU. Its Education Department (0171 420 9894) produces good materials, including a Poetry Pack. Membership available for schools.

Young Book Trust, Book House, 45 East Hill, London SW18 2QZ. An independent charity, this is the children's book division of Book Trust. Aims to be a focus for activity, promotional and book-related material, and an information exchange. Produces annual listing of 100 Best Books.

School Library Association, Liden Library, Barrington Close, Liden, Swindon SN3 6HF.

READERSHIP AWARD

Awarded to: _____

For excellent response to ~

_____

by _____

Signed _____

Date _____

Have you seen the companion volume to *Reading Alive?*

Library Alive!
Promoting reading and research in the school library

An invaluable resource book for the teacher and librarian, Library Alive! is packed with challenging and absorbing activities to help children learn the skills they need to become confident, independent readers and borrowers – above all to enjoy using books.

It includes games and activities to encourage critical and evaluative skills, research using many kinds of books and resources, and a knowledge of the organisation of a library. The 'planner' and 'skills index' make this book particularly helpful for non-specialists.

The book contains resource and activity material which may be photocopied and distributed for classroom use.